Reiki Plus® *Natural Healing*

a

Spiritual Guide to

Reiki Plus®

by

David G. Jarrell

Reiki Master

Founder of the

Reiki Plus System of Natural Healing

and the

Reiki Plus®*Institute*

at

Hibernia West
Rt 3 Box 313
Celina, Tennessee 38551
(615) 243-3712

First Edition, September 27, 1984
Second Edition, April 14, 1988
Third Edition, January 11, 1990
Fourth Edition, September 4, 1991

DEDICATION

Dedicated to the Aquarian Age, the Reiki Ray, and the work of the Arcturian Children upon this planet Earth, who by attunement to St. Germain and the Brotherhood of Light shall transmute The Ego Power Struggle to a state of Spiritual Integrity of Power directed by Universal Divine Love.

This Fourth Edition is further dedicated to all of the students who have made this Fourth Edition needed as a Healing Guide for the students yet unknown to them, and by their design have played an instrumental part in the timeliness of the event. We are grateful to all present in the healing field, both physical and spiritual.

Note of thanks to the following people:

Editor:
Richard Leavitt

Art:
Charisse
Rosie Voreadou
Diane McKinnis (back cover)
Kelly Jarrell (front cover)

Typing of book:
Judy Gomez (1st Edition)
David Jarrell (2-4th Editions)

Special Thanks

The author hopes this *Reiki Plus Natural Healing* manual will be a useful tool in your use of Reiki Natural Healing. We have striven to present many useful approaches for your needs as a beginning student. The *Reiki Plus Institute* where serious students can extend and deepen their practical concepts of healing, presents additional material in the *Reiki Plus Professional Practitioner's Manual* (publication date set for January 1992). This material and the Techniques devised by David G. Jarrell are available to all students who desire to pursue the 500 hour *Professional Practitioner's Certification Program* taught by the faculty of the *Reiki Plus Institute*.

We wish to thank all students for their feedback, which has been used to update this edition. We are always pleased to receive your written and telephone comment and experiences in Reiki.

The terms "I AM Christ-Consciousness" and "Christ-Consciousness" are used throughout this book solely as a reference of the higher consciousness ascribed to enlightened souls, i.e., Buddha, Jesus, et al. The statement is in no way intended to imply a statement of religious ideology. It is the belief of the author that all souls are from a single Deity and have the ability and the desire to attain a consciousness ascribed to these enlightened souls; who, in physical body, have transcended the ego of human personality and truly are illumined in Universal and Unconditional Love and hold the Grace of Forgiveness in their countenance. The author is the founding minister of the Pyramids of Light Inc., a non-denominational Christian Church, dedicated to the laws of Natural Healing and the Teachings of Jesus the Christ and the truths taught in the Holy Bible. The *Reiki Plus Institute* is the educational arm of the Church for legal certification of Professional Practitioner's and required training for Ordination in the four levels of the Ministry.

A very special thanks to my wife Kelly Ryan Jarrell for the moral, physical and spiritual support to make this commitment to His work more easily accomplished and for being my mirror in my growth through the trails of human reality. Last and not least a special thanks to my daughters Samantha and Heather, who teach me more through their wisdom and continued connection with the Divine Angelic Kingdom of God than any book I have ever read or person I have met.

My thanks to the faculty of the *Reiki Plus Institute*, present and future, who have spent the many years to provide to the student of natural healing an opportunity to reach his or her dreams and to become a highly trained Natural Health Care Provider. The effort and energy that has made this Institute available to the student can never be known, but fortunately the benefits of the combined labor can and will be an influence upon the consciousness of humanity, as the graduates of the *Reiki Plus Institute* address the Natural Healing needs of our society world wide.

An Invitation to You, the Student of Reiki

If you are reading this book and have not yet experienced the teachings of the *Reiki Plus Institute* because a teacher lives far away from you, know that your wish is but a phone call away. We are always pleased when you call and inquire about a class near where you live or to discuss how you can become a sponsor of a class and pay for your education at the same time.

Our teachers travel and present our curriculum in cities and towns around the USA and Europe, sponsored by people just like you, who desire to learn *Reiki Plus* and then realize they desire to become certified as a *Professional Practitioner of Reiki Plus*. The two year program is discussed at the end of this book and a catalog of our complete curriculum can be ordered for $3.00 from the Institute's National Headquarters, Hibernia West, Rt 3 Box 313, Celina, Tennessee 38551.

The founder and director is the author, and I am always pleased to receive your phone call (615) 243-3712 between normal business hours (9am - 6pm CST) or your letter. If I am away teaching be sure to talk to Kelly or Heather, of course when we are not home the answer machine is. We look forward to meeting you personally in a class, if we have not yet had the pleasure.

TABLE OF CONTENTS

Introduction: *Reiki Plus* Natural Healing 5
Comments for the Fourth Edition. 6
The *Reiki Plus* Institute. 6
The "I AM" Invocation. 7

CHAPTERS

1. HISTORICAL PHILOSOPHY
Symbols Of *Reiki Plus* 8
The Reiki Ray 9
The Legend Of Reiki 11
The Five Spiritual Principals Of *Reiki Plus* .14
The Two Precepts Of *Reiki Plus* 18
The Initiations 18
The Three Degrees (Four Levels) Of *Reiki Plus*. 19
The Twenty-One Days of Initiation 20
The Twenty-One Day Healing Cycle. 21

2. LEGAL
Healing And The Law 22
Guideline Of Contract For Healing 22

3. DIAGRAMS
Chakras 24
Creative Sacral Distributor. 28
Endocrine System 29
Chart Of Effects Of Spinal Misalignments 30

4. UNDERSTANDING HOW DISEASE AND HEALING MANIFEST
"Pandora's Box" - The "Tumbleweed Theory" 31
The Predisposition To Wellness 32
Wellness: Walking In Meditation 34
Be Willing To Speak, Be Willing To Listen 35
Communicating Truth - Becoming Light 36
Closing The Throat - "The Causal Factor" 38
Stress: The Unqualified Energy 39

5. THE HEALING PROCEDURES
Attunement: The *Reiki Plus* Treatment 41
Attunement To The Healee's Pain 41
Know You Are Light 42
The Healing Setting 43
The Healing Curve 46

6. FASTING 50

7. THE TREATMENT: HAND POSITIONS AND DIAGRAMS
Treating Oneself 53
Treating Others 60
Special Positions for Specific Imbalances 66
Sequence of Healing Session 73
Polarity Positions For Running Reiki Energy 74

This healing manual presents the modality of *Reiki Plus* Natural Healing, a spiritual, esoteric, divine metaphysical approach to understanding the behavior of psycho-physical disorders, and to serve as a basis for your progress towards being a *Reiki Plus* Practitioner.

We hope that you will want to learn all of the dimensions influencing human existence so as to live in a balanced, harmonious and loving state of well-being. Every individual soul returning to the planet Earth has done so to learn how to become effective in this process: soul existence in the physical body. In this healing manual you will be presented many concepts considered essential to personally achieve self-healing. When these concepts become thoroughly incorporated into your emotional and thought process, you will be better prepared to help others in need of healing.

Throughout this manual you will read the pronoun "We." This manual could not have been possible without the inspiration given to the author by the Brotherhood of Light, which includes the Master Healer Jesus the Christ. "I AM" grateful to their continued support, in the completion of the Fourth Edition. It would have been very easy for the pen to have continued forming their thoughts on paper; however, the manual would never reach a state of completion. No doubt as new insight is gained, this edition will be revised and expanded.

In writing this healing guide, I had to acknowledge that *Reiki Plus* reaches out to embrace a vast amount of essential data, more than can be thoroughly covered in the present design of the First Degree *Reiki Plus* class. Also, that to become thoroughly efficient in the use of the energy from the Reiki Ray with the modality of *Reiki Plus*, the healer needs to make a commitment to his or her soul growth. This is not only personal dedication to be of service to humanity, it is to be a servant to the "I AM" consciousness, to know that we are a spark of God, a soul journeying home.

Students desiring to continue to higher Initiations in *Reiki Plus* Natural healing will have to understand the fundamental principles presented in this text. The scope and depth of the material presented herein is the foundation of all the Degrees of Initiation in *Reiki Plus*. What must be realized is that Reiki is a healing energy from God and that *Reiki Plus* is a modality: a philosophical approach to effect a total healing of the Mind, Body, and Emotions; the spiritual teachings of Dr. Usui. In times of doubt and personal struggle and trails, Dr. Usui has spiritually supported the author, helping me to reach beyond the perceived limitations of the challenge. To help me maintain the **Spiritual Integrity of Reiki.**

In the last one hundred years our civilization has been irradiated with transformative cosmic and galactic influences at a degree of intensity which mankind has only begun to even conceive. The desperate attempt to hold on to the old conventions, the Saturnian influence of rigid and restricting limitations, the "concrete foundations of proven success" is being threatened. Humanity is having the old flooring ripped out from under it, for the days of Saturnian isolationism are over. Our planet is receiving galactic energy through the planets Uranus, Neptune, and Pluto, and we must be mobile to flow with the changes. For **change** is the **"constant factor"** effecting humankind and our environment every moment of existence.

Be then in the flow of transformation, Be in The Light.

Comments for the Fourth Edition

It is with great excitement that I come to the next stage of *Reiki Plus* , the Fourth Edition of the healing manual. As I look back over the years which brought about the First Edition in 1984, it becomes clear that *Reiki Plus* continues to expand.

Each class that we teach brings me closer to the realization that the teachings of Master Jesus must be made a more complete part of *Reiki Plus*, not in the religious sense, but in the Spiritual essence which Dr. Usui sought in his journey to find how Master Jesus healed. **Reiki** means **"the Spiritual Power of God."** It is the indwelling "power" that awaits awakening in each of us. *Reiki Plus* is a means to make personal contact with the "God Within", so that we will recognize the "God around us."

The recognition of the "God Self" is first attained after the "Christ Self" is illuminated. This is not a mental recognition; it is a process of living the **Five Spiritual Principles of Reiki Plus**. The teachings of Master Jesus came through His Christ Consciousness just as Dr. Usui's came from embracing His. Each of us walks the earth plane in human form, however, we are not limited to this realm.

For our journey is the embracing of the "Divine Self" and expanding our consciousness as we journey through the lessons of the personality towards physical reunion with "soul." It is the transformative action of the personality which is the true vehicle of soul consciousness. The experiences of the personality in this journey begin to produce a positive accumulation of knowledge when the lessons shown by the planet Pluto in our natal horoscope and its transits are greeted with a positive attitude and a surrendering heart.

It is at this point that we truly begin healing the personality and reaching out to find our "Christ Consciousness", so that we can be embraced by our "Christ Self." It is our sincere hopes that your journey "home" be enhanced by the words written and even more so by the words implied within this text.

  The *Reiki Plus Institute*

We, the Teachers of the *Reiki Plus Institute*, invite you to step into world and community service by completing your Natural Health Care Education in the field of Functional Energy Healing. *Reiki Plus* teaches the practitioner how to align the mind, body and emotions of the client to promote spiritual wholeness and wellbeing. Functional Energy training is compatible with Structural Body Work and other Natural Healing systems and healing techniques. *Reiki Plus* is based on the teaching concept of presenting a continuity of *Divine Metaphysical* knowledge to each student in an individualized manner, founding a comprehensive integration of the teachings. This will lead the student to his or her own wisdom and understanding of man's ability to heal with God's divine light.

The Institute's 500 credit hour *Professional Practitioner's Certification Program* spans seven curriculum areas with 11 specific approaches of Functional Healing Techniques. courses 100 - 300 are all required plus 85 hours of 400-600 level courses for graduation. The *objective* of our program is to provide training to the aspiring Practitioner in the spiritual and technical aspects of a Natural Health Care Provider.

Our concept is to approach the client in a scientific manner from a spiritual and holistic consciousness, thereby providing a clear and methodical program of treatment for the needs of the individual. Throughout this course of study you will be taught the four aspects of healing so that your client's will achieve the desired state of Wellness.

A *Reiki Plus Practitioner* is taught to embrace the grace and reward of being an instrument of God upon the planet Earth, knowing and living the art of healing, where:
"God's Light and Love surrounds you; God's Light and Love fills you; God's Light and Love radiates through you. That you, as an instrument of Light, know peace, Joy and the Art of Surrender. That you are a clear healing agent like the rainbow: Opalescent with the teachings of the Master's. Radiant in the transfiguration of the Christed energy, Humble in your service to God's divine plan.

Our foundation courses, **Reiki 101 and 202** are recognized and co-sponsored by the University of Iowa School of Nursing, for which CEU's are awarded. Many other states have followed suit and allow Registered Nurse's to be awarded CEU's. Nurses have also been reimbursed by their employing Institution for the Institute's courses.

For more information see the appendix at the end of this book and you are invited to call for more information about classes near you and to order our Catalog. The Catalog of the Institutes complete curriculum can be ordered by sending a check for only $3.00 to:

The *Reiki Plus Institute*, Rt 3 Box 313, Celina, TN 38551 (615) 243-3712

THE "I AM" INVOCATION

During the Piscean Age, God gave man two Commandments to understand and to incorporate into his consciousness:

Love the Lord thy God with all thy Heart,
with all thy Soul,
and with all thy Mind.

Love thy neighbor as thyself;

In the Aquarian Age, humankind must activate these laws on all levels of consciousness to awaken God Consciousness.

An awakening of this vibration can be achieved by saying the "I AM" Invocation out loud. It is helpful to say before meditation, as it sets the stage for attuning to one's purpose on the planet.

For the full effect to take place within your Mind, Body, and Emotions for Spiritual balancing, it is important that the "I AM" be stated with reverence. Feel the vibrations of the "I AM THAT I AM" resonating through your Mind, Body, and Emotions each time you begin each line with the "I AM." Do not be in a hurry. Be in the totality of the moment. Become the "I AM" that you are and that you will be.

This prayer of invocation was channelled December 9, 1982 through David G. Jarrell. It is not be confused with the Great Invocation published by Lucis Trust from the works of A.A. Bailey.

I AM the point of Light within the mind of God,
I AM the Light descended upon the Earth.
I AM the Love within the heart of God,
I AM the Love descended into the hearts of humankind.

Let Light and Love stream forth
and awaken the I AM within all humankind.

I AM the centre where the Will of God is known,
I AM the purpose to guide the Wills of men,
I AM reaches out and receives from the Masters,
I AM becomes the servant of the Masters:
and from within to abound with the will of God.

I AM the centre of the race of humankind,
I AM the Plan of Light and Love
and through the I AM will Light and Love prevail.

I AM the Light and Love and Power,and only
I AM can restore the Plan on Earth.

REIKI PLUS® ~ the spiritual power of God

REI

KI

PLUS®

Chapter One

THE REIKI RAY

Reiki, or **Reiki Plus**®, is **not a religion**; it is a healing energy from God. It involves no doctrines, creeds or contradictions to the Universal Laws of Spiritual Consciousness and Unconditional Love. No matter where a person may be at any point in his life, Reiki will harmonize and embrace his philosophical center point, adding to it the Divine Presence. Reiki opens the heart to expand the holographic sphere of our love consciousness.

Reiki is part of the Emerald Ray, and is served under the direction of the Reiki Masters in spirit. They direct the healing and initiatory energy of Reiki. Once the individual is attuned to Reiki through initiations, he is permanently connected to the Reiki energy. To "turn on" the Reiki healing energy the initiate needs not alter his consciousness. He only needs to "think Reiki" and allow the energy to flow into him from God and then out of his hands. Meditation, prayer and imaging does assist many persons in centering their conscious mind to open the higher self to being an instrument of healing.

Simply placing one's hands on oneself, or another person, and opening to the flow of the Reiki energy, allows this energy to flow through the individual. It fills the healer's body first and then flows out from the heart through the healer's hands into the individual who is receiving the healing.

Reiki energy comes from God through the Brotherhood of Light, the Masters of the Seven Rays, to the Reiki hierarchy itself. There are, for each of the Ten levels of human initiation, Rays (specific bands of colors surrounding an individual's head, often seen without clairvoyance) through which we must pass. Persons Initiated into the Reiki Ray quickly illumine and attune to the Fifth Ray of Truth. This is an extremely powerful healing energy. It is one of the few forms of healing that can be used to heal oneself.

Reiki will either **give or take away** the proper amount of energy needed to balance the Mind, Body and emotions. It will effect change in the chemical structure of the body, helping to rebuild muscles, nerves, skeletal structure, and regenerating organs. It will provide the energy to balance and straighten the spine. It will change anything that needs to be changed within the physical and etheric organism.

Reiki healing is a pure energy form. When it is combined with the sincere desire of the healee, who is willing to effect a cleansing within his or her emotional and spiritual consciousness, a total healing occurs.

We must always remember that the energy of the God-Force is neutral and awaits positive, productive empowerment by the healee. The healer plays an instrumental part in transformation, and yet, ultimately it is up to the healee to manifest harmony and balance in his or her own life.

The healer is a channel and must not allow his "Ego-Will" to desire the healee well. A healer must be a clear vessel through which the Reiki Ray flows. This allows the highest Soul purpose to be the outcome of the healing. Then no karmic debt can be incurred by the desire of the healer's own ego.

Healing is effected when the healer can allow Divine Will to replace his own Will, so that he truly feels "Thy Will Be Done, Not Mine." This will allow healing to reach the "highest soul purpose" for the healee, rather than having his ego desire dictate through control and fear, limiting the healing process. The personality needs be in total alignment with "Thy Will", which is achieved through the act of surrendering the "little me consciousness" and trusting in the "God-self."

Dr. Mikao Usui

Dr. Usui dedicated his life to the teaching of Ancient Truth. Without his disciplined perseverance, we might not have the blessing of the Reiki Ray. Our lives will be enriched from his labor of Love for humankind. His dedication as a Servant of the Light continues to shine upon our Spiritual path in Reiki.

(February 7, 1802 until October 16, 1883, unconfirmed dates)

THE STORY OF REIKI

It is believed that in the year 1822 in the city of Kyoto, Japan, Dr. Mikao Usui, a Buddhist monk, began a twenty-eight year search during which he rediscovered how the Buddha had healed. Before Jesus, the Buddha had possessed the gift of healing through Divine Love and the human touch.

Dr. Usui's journey began by visiting and asking the different Buddhist sects if they could perform the miracles that Buddha performed: could they heal the body? The Buddhists felt that healing of the Spirit and healing of the body were not always directly connected. They concentrated on the Spirit, and not on the body. They felt that the body and the Spirit were separate and that the Spirit was what needed to be healed. They left the healing of the body to medical doctors.

Dr. Usui finally went to a Zen monastery. He asked the same question of the senior monk: "Do Zen monks and priests know how to heal the body?" The monk answered, "Not any more." Dr. Usui was puzzled by his answer. "What do you mean not any more?" The Zen monk explained that they had been concentrating so heavily on healing the Spirit they had forgotten how to heal the body.

The monk felt that if Dr. Usui's destiny was to rediscover how the Buddha had healed the body, it would unfold before him. So Dr. Usui asked if he might stay and study at the Zen monastery in Kyoto. He was accepted, for all people who desire mastery were accepted in their quest.

And so, under the guidance of the Zen monk, Dr. Usui began meditating, reading the sutras, the writings and teachings of the Buddha. He read the Japanese translation over a period of several years, but did not find a suitable answer. As he had so often done, he went back to the monk and asked for guidance. The monk said that he should meditate, for in meditation he would find the answer within.

Through his meditations, Dr. Usui was guided to learn Chinese and began to read the sutras in Chinese. After a few years Dr. Usui had still not uncovered what he felt were the essential teaching or keys to healing. Again, guided by meditation, Dr. Usui was directed to learn the language of Tibetan. "The Buddha (Siddhartha Gautama) (563-483 B.C.) was a prince of the Sakya tribe, born at Kapila-vastu near the border between present -day Nepal and India. After his enlightenment, at the age of 35, he spent 45 years traveling and preaching in northern India. His teachings were taken down in Sanskrit and Pali, carried to china in 645 A.D. The Tibetan priest translated the Sanskrit to Tibetan." (Richard Leavitt, editor of 3rd Edition, 1989.)

In a few years Dr. Usui mastered the Tibetan language and began reading the teachings of the Tibetan Buddhist Sect. In the Tibetan Buddhist writings, Dr. Usui discovered what he felt to be the keys to healing. The Tibetan priest were taught through meditation and channeling radiated by the Brotherhood of Light.

*   *   *

As has been from all times, the Truth has radiated from the God-Force to humankind. Many teachers have been the receivers of this Truth, as many are now and will be in the days ahead. This imparted knowledge continues to be channeled to those who will receive and take the teachings beyond the Self.

The Reiki healing comes through the Brotherhood of Light. These teachers of the Brotherhood are a focus of the God-Force. Names have been given to them so humankind will be clear about their words, actions and deeds. The Healing Ray, a focus of Emerald Light, is called the Fifth Ray, one of the Ten Rays of God's radiant messages for human initiation. An Ascended Tibetan Master has maintained the Reiki Ray focus for humankind since the beginning, and is now assisted by Dr. Usui.

*   *   *

Dr. Usui, realizing that he had possibly found the keys to healing, went back to the monk to tell him of his exciting discovery and ask his advice. "Now that I have found what I have been looking for, how do I know that it is correct and, if so, how do I use it?"

Through meditation, he and the monk were told that he should go to a holy mountain north of Kyoto called Kurama-yama. On Kurama-yama he was to meditate and fast for twenty-one days; during this time he would receive enlightenment and spiritual clarity.

Dr. Usui gathered up a few belongings and made his pilgrimage from Kyoto to Kurama-yama. He climbed the mountain and found a location facing east. Every morning he awakened before the sun rose and threw away one of the twenty-one stones he had placed in front of his meditation spot to keep count of the days.

Each day he meditated and fasted. On the twenty-first day, Dr. Usui awakened to a darkened morning. It was like a new moon day, when no light shone in the heavens before the breaking of dawn. When he awakened he could not see even his hand in front of his face. He found his way to his meditation spot and picked up the last stone. Dr. Usui prayed before throwing the last stone off the side of the mountain. He asked for confirmation of his findings and asked to be given the enlightenment of how to use it.

As he threw the stone off the side of the mountain, a light appeared far off in the east. It began getting brighter and coming closer to him. It frightened him and he wanted to run away. He heard himself say, "You have searched for twenty-one years and you have meditated and fasted for twenty-one days. You have asked for enlightenment and confirmation, and now you want to run away from it?" And so, Dr. Usui quieted his intellect and said, "No, if that light is for me, I accept the enlightenment." The light became very bright and streamed across the heavens to open his third eye.

He thought he had died and had ascended into heaven. He had never before been in such a euphoric state. His entire field of vision was a rainbow of color. Out of the rainbow came bubbles of gold, white, blue, and violet. Each of the different bubbles contained symbolic messages. A voice said, "**These are the keys to healing; learn them, do not forget them; and, do not allow them to be lost.**"

Dr. Usui saw the bubbles and heard the voice . . . until finally, he heard himself speak out in his own mind, "I have them; I will not forget them; and I will not allow them to be lost." Then he awakened and realized he was still on the Earth. Gathering his wits and belongings, he hurriedly began walking down the mountain. He was excited; he was energized. He wanted to get back to the monk to tell him what had happened.

Along the way, Dr. Usui stubbed his toe. He bent down and took his toe in his hand. To his excitement the pain and the bleeding stopped very rapidly. He realized that something was different about the energy from his hands; they became very hot. After healing his toe, Dr. Usui continued his way down the mountain. Soon he began to feel hungry. He stopped at a home that served travelers, and ordered cold rice and cold tea. The owner said, "Oh, sir monk, I can see that you have been fasting and meditating for many days. I think you should have warm rice and warm tea, so that you will not get sick."

Dr. Usui thanked him, and asked for his order of cold rice and tea.

In a few moments a Japanese girl, with a bandage wrapped around her jaw and her head, brought Dr. Usui his meal. Dr. Usui asked, "What is wrong?" She told him that she had a toothache. Encouraged by his own phenomenal pain relief, Dr. Usui asked, "May I give you a healing?" She accepted his offer gladly. So, Dr. Usui put his hands around the girl's jaw and within a short period of time the pain and swelling started going down. She was very happy and went off to tell her father.

After Dr. Usui had eaten his meal of cold rice and cold tea, he wanted to pay the father. He reached into his pocket to get out some coins but the father said, "Thank you, sir monk, but I cannot accept the money. You have rendered unto my daughter a service for which I do not have the money to pay. Please accept the food in exchange for the healing service that you rendered."

Dr. Usui accepted the food in exchange for his service as a healing channel.

He continued his walk back to Kyoto. When he arrived at the monastery, he went in to tell the monk what had happened. He asked for advice on what he should do now that he had received the keys and the energy of healing. He wanted to learn more about its use and to how to develop it. Dr. Usui was directed by the monk to meditate.

From the meditation he was directed to go into Kyoto to heal the poor. Dr. Usui thought this an excellent idea, and prepared to go the next day. He was excited by this challenge.

For the next seven years, Dr. Usui gave healings from early morning to late at night. Dr. Usui was very disciplined and dedicated. He healed the young and the old alike, seeing many beautiful results take place. He began to understand how Reiki flowed through him into the healee, and how the body becomes well.

One afternoon Dr. Usui took a walk. While standing on the street corner, he saw a young beggar who looked very familiar, but he said to himself, "I do not know him: I do not know any beggars of that age that look like him."

Finally, Dr. Usui asked if the beggar knew him, and the man said, "Of course Dr. Usui, I know you. Do you not remember me? I am one of the first persons that you ever healed."

Dr. Usui said, "I healed you and you are still a beggar?"

The man looked back at him and said, "Oh, Dr. Usui, yes, and I did just what you told me. I went out to the temple to receive a name, went into society and began dealing with my karma, doing just what you told me to do. I even got a job and soon married, but it was too much responsibility. So, I decided that I would rather be a beggar. That way I would not even have to be responsible for myself."

Dr. Usui turned around without continuing the conversation and returned to his room. Picking up his belongings, he began his journey back to the monastery. As he walked back to the monastery he was greeted in Spirit by the teachers who had greeted him on Kurama-yama. They bestowed upon him understanding of two very important elements: healing of the Spirit and the responsibility of the healee in the healing process. Dr. Usui realized that he had done the reverse of the Buddhists by concentrating on healing the body and not the Spirit. He was, at this time, given the **Five Spiritual Principles of Reiki** by the Teachers in Spirit.

The Five Spiritual Principles created significant changes in the subsequent healings that Dr. Usui performed. He realized that he had been giving healing away without requiring the healee to take any **responsibility** whatsoever. Also, there had not been an **exchange of energy** for the **services rendered**. The new teachings provided Spiritual concepts to be integrated with the physical aspect of the Reiki energy.

* * *

Dr. Usui realized that living these Spiritual Principles would effect changes in his life and in the healing of others. He observed how the healer's energy (auric field) influences the etheric bodies (the true chakra location) of the healee. Not only did this subtle energy alter the healee's consciousness, it paralleled the healing of the physical body.

Dr. Usui also learned, that as the Reiki healer grew through applying the Spiritual Principles on a day-to-day basis, their essence was manifested on all levels of his life. The way in which a person acted, responded, understood and provided advice to himself and others was changed from the "I-Ego-Power" to the Divine Will of the "I AM" consciousness.

This development created, and still does create, transformations of consciousness, for Reiki is from the heart. It is only through the heart that the fullness of life can be known. The heart is the doorway of Love of the Self, the Christ and the God within, and the outpouring of Divine Love. From the abundance of God-fulfilling love presence, we can love our fellow brothers and sisters and come to know the true meaning of Unconditional Love.

* * *

From this point Dr. Usui taught Reiki throughout the islands of Japan until his transition about 1883. During the years from 1850 until 1883, Dr. Usui gathered a following of sixteen teachers. Before his transition he asked Dr. Hayashi to see that the teachings were preserved.

Dr. Hayashi went on to start the first established Reiki clinic in Tokyo. To ensure that Reiki would survive the forthcoming Second World War, he decided to train two women. His inner vision had guided this action, for he felt that

most of the males would be called to serve their country.

Dr. Hayashi's insight proved correct. Fortunately the two women, Hawayo Takata and another, a Japanese national, did survive the war. Takata, who lived in Hawaii, was instrumental in spreading the teachings of Reiki to the United States and Canada. The other teacher remained in Japan.

Takata, a Reiki Master, passed on her gifts of Reiki to many students, some of whom were Initiated as Masters. Takata transitioned on December 11, 1980. As was the custom, she did not appoint any of her student/Masters to be in charge of the Reiki Teachings, knowing that each would follow his or her own heart.

Many Reiki Masters have extended the method of Reiki by adding their own areas of specialization to the basic Reiki technique. By incorporating Metaphysical, Esoteric, Spiritual and Holistic teachings, they hope to enrich the student's training. This is, and will continue to be, the direction of Reiki to embrace the unlimited sphere of Macro-Micro cosmic attunement to healing and to leave no valuable approach in the creation of wellness for humankind un-turned or not inspected. Healing must draw from the infinite resources of God. Humankind is the co-creative instrument of the universe through which God channels inspiration for the creation of Divine processes of healing.

Ultimately, wellness is Spirit in flesh charged with Holy Breath taking full responsibility for free will choice. This is the aim of the teachings of Dr. Usui, and it is also the aim of the author.

The author, the founder of the **Reiki Plus®** Institute and Natural Healing modality of **Reiki Plus®**, is the 24th Reiki Master in the lineage of Masters, trained under Virginia Samdahl from First degree into Mastership training. Mastership training completed found the author in philosophical conflict with his teacher, which led to his Mastership initiation by Barbara McCullough on August 5, 1981 and later initiation by Phyllis Furumoto, Takata's granddaughter in the month of November 1981.

THE FIVE SPIRITUAL PRINCIPLES OF Reiki Plus®

JUST FOR TODAY, I SHALL TRUST

All things happen in accordance with the Divine and Universal plan. If my mind is attuned, the highest "soul purpose" will be my objective. I will then glean my thoughts to harvest my day-to-day enlightenment. I will know worrying interferes by creating illogical reasoning through irrational deductive patterns of thought, establishing limitations and separation from my "I AM" Christ consciousness. I will accept the voice within and the unlimited potential of my God Presence, which awaits my awakening to the acknowledgement of oneness. Therefore, I will not interfere with the Universal timing of life; I will attune myself to the synchronicity of events; I shall be willing to hear the inner voice of the God Presence; and then, I will know there is no need to worry.

If we are conscious of all that we have to be thankful for, then we have no time to worry about that which isn't.

"Just for today." Today is the present moment and it is the future. If we live today without worry, then tomorrow shall be transformed in the peace of our Divineness.

To worry is to be unsure of God's role in our lives; it is not trusting that all things happen with Divine Purpose. We will grow to a higher state of awareness and enlightenment through surrendering to our Divine Plan.

When someone else enters our life path, be it day or night, God has sent that person to us. God knows that either we have the ability to help him, to be a loving listener or to learn from the experience.

Worry only prevents attunement and awareness to our purpose upon the planet. It keeps us out of the flow of the I AM PRESENCE. All actions are Divine and bring us closer to the Light. Acknowledge that you have the opportunity for growth, awareness, love, and compassion.

JUST FOR TODAY, I SHALL DO MY WORK HONESTLY

I love myself enough to realize that all I do affects others. If I do not work at my highest potential, then I am not being honest with myself or society. I am not an isolated entity living in a separate microcosmic world. "I AM" is a part of all parts. How I see myself reflects my joy in being a part of the sum, a totality of the all; and therefore, to be honest with myself is to love myself enough to do unto others as I wish them to do unto me.

Doing one's work honestly means being truthful to the God-Self. Being in tune with what you are doing creates harmony; creating harmony allows you to be doing what is productive for society, yourself, and all of God's creation. Therefore, honesty is alignment with the purpose of the Divine Plan of planet Earth.

We are all a particle of Light from the same Source. What we think and how we work directly affects all levels of the Cosmos. We are a part of a Greater whole. Fulfillment of the Divine Plan comes only when we put forth constructive, loving energy.

On a more intimate level, how you perform your daily work task directly affects the overall objectives of the company that employs you or the organization that you have agreed to support. The Law of Karma is, "What we sow, so shall we reap." If we sow positive, productive, loving energy, we receive the same energy returned tenfold or more. If we put out negative energy, then we reap negative results tenfold or more. Our state of harmony or disharmony directly affects every situation in our life. So, create a healthy state of existence through doing your work honestly.

Every moment of the day God provides us lessons which may be seen as confrontations. We can use these lessons to learn to balance our physical needs and desires toward a more spiritually attuned state. To establish balance, we must have our feet on the ground, our head in the Heavens, and our arms outstretched. When this process is firmly established in our conscious mind, we can direct ourselves to maintain an earthly and spiritual state of balance and harmony. Confrontations are not problems; they are opportunities to work toward a spiritual manner of living. To be spiritual is to be conscious of the needs of the Self and of the needs of others. To first be conscious of our own needs, we must love ourselves. Unless we can love ourselves, we cannot begin to love God and experience God's Divine Love. We can only love another to the degree we love ourselves, which is the degree to which we acknowledge the God Within us, of and made in the Divine Image, carrying the same potential, desiring to manifest itself in our everyday life.

Because most people have not yet perceived the distinction between truth and illusion, they see existence through eyes of limited consciousness, unaware of the micro-macro cosmic relationship of humankind. Love is the key to becoming aware of the higher levels of consciousness. It is hard to believe that we simply came to planet Earth to live and die without reason. God's Divine Plan for humankind on this planet is to expand our spiritual essence along the path by which we proceed toward perfection.

It is important to realize that life's tasks are those lessons not yet mastered. Mastery comes from honest effort to clearly understand what is involved in the completion and accomplishment of each level of growth. We must be willing to fly into the center of the flame and be consumed by the Initiation of Fire. Then we will transmute the Karmic lesson, the "ever present future," and reach a state of mastery. Life is a simple process; the human personality (I-Egoism) has made it a complex Maya of intellectual dichotomies. Maya questions the illusion of reality versus the reality of the illusion? For additional information see Ponder on This, published by Lucis Trust on the works of Master Djwhal Khul and Alice A. Bailey.

JUST FOR TODAY, I SHALL ACCEPT MY MANY BLESSINGS

I shall consider myself **worthy to receive** all that God has to offer me; to love myself enough to receive, unrestricted, the Divine gifts from God; to create the self-image of worthiness, being united rather than separate, a part of the whole, worthy of all gifts. I shall recognize that God's gifts often come through human sources, and therefore see the God-presence in all men. I shall utilize these blessings creatively for the benefit of humankind, not just for self. I shall develop the God-presence through the Christ Consciousness in all my actions in order to know the higher spiritual perfect Self made manifest on the human personality level of my existence. I shall be responsive to the Divine gift of creativity as my purpose of life, without manifesting thoughts of unworthiness. I shall become an instrument of God's prosperity: a Light, shining for the world to see, and show thanks for my many blessings.

The key to creativity is your ability to visualize. If you can imagine it happening, so it shall be. This is the process of directing energy from the visual state into the state of reality , accepting that it is going to happen and giving thanks to God for His blessings in helping us create it. What you think, **IS**; for it becomes your reality.

We must also be aware of the hundredfold gifts that God has provided for us. Look around you. Look within you. You are a magical instrument of Divine Creation. We are His Light upon this planet and He offers us the opportunity to grow within His Light and blessings. He only asks that we be true to ourselves in asking; being true to ourselves is being true to God. Many people feel that they have little, if anything, for which to be thankful. It is important to know what you are asking for in your request. Let's look at this situation dealing with work, success, and a high paying job.

Many people say, "I want a job paying a lot of money." Instead, say, "I want a job that will give me the creative expression of my abilities, the harmony of working relationships with people and the environment, the expressions of myself, the contentment and feeling of being in tune, and a job that will provide an adequate return of income as the reward for the energy I put out."

When you are clear with yourself and have an understanding of your intent, then you will feel the blessings returned from your effort to achieve your goal. Remember, we always receive what we ask for, so be sure you really know what you are asking God to give you, and if you are really willing to live up to the request.

JUST FOR TODAY, I SHALL BE AT PEACE

I shall not allow my ego to be affected by my desires and expectations. If I allow my ego to get in the way, I have not realized that the situation is a mirror, a reflection of cause and effect created by me.

To yield to anger is to desire control. It is the unwillingness to see what about myself I do not like. Anger only serves to limit awareness and creates unhappiness that can lead to physical and emotional afflictions.

When we are not angry, we understand the synchronization of "interplaying", of receiving what we have put out. Other persons involved in synchronistic interplay are also there to learn, even though they are not the cause of our own imbalanced emotional anger. Anger only limits the growth, understanding and awareness which can be learned from "interplaying." To effect change, the "I" ("with Thine Eye, so shall thou see) must be willing to see and hear the actions of the ego.

Anger is life force energy directed into a course of noncreative nonproductiveness. So, when you feel the emotion of anger (hurt), stop! Then say, with sincerity and intent: "Thank you God for the opportunity of this awareness (insert your emotion), that I can now become a master over this emotion." When you allow yourself to **surrender** to the highest soul purpose behind each event in your life, you make a quantum leap in awareness. You have experienced your higher consciousness, your **"Eye"** to your Spiritual Self.

Energy is the essence of life. Misdirected energy, such as anger, is received by people, rooms, food, and all living forms in our environment. It must be converted to a state of harmony or it will affect anyone entering such a contaminated room or eating contaminated food.

If you enter a disharmonious environment or meet an angry person, do not "buy into" that state of disharmony. The "Mirror Effect" is a very powerful tool; "a smile will create a smile, love will radiate love in return." The choice in life is yours. Feeling the inner trigger of emotions which spark anger is normal. We are still human and still are learning to free ourselves from being controlled by our physical/mental emotions. Holding on to anger is being unable to rise up to your "I AM" consciousness and to free yourself from your emotions, desires, and cravings to have it "your way."

A very powerful technique for not reacting to negative energy in the environment or from another person is touching your tongue to a pressure point inside your mouth. Put the tip of your tongue lightly against the center ridge on the roof of the mouth about one quarter inch behind your front teeth. This will balance the Left and Right hemispheres of the brain. This balances you. You will radiate loving energy and a smiling face, and will be unable to speak undesirable words (while your tongue is touching the roof of your mouth, of course). As you are radiating this energy of love, think the colors golden-white and pink. Golden-white is the color of the Christ-Self and pink the color of Universal Love. Feel these colors and their harmonious energy radiating within you, surrounding you, and then entering the other person's aura. This will convert his energy to a state of peace, harmony, joy, and love. Others in your auric (energy) field will also experience this healing. Remember, you have the ever constant opportunity to heal your environment, to live in loving peace with all creation. This is a challenge, our goal as human beings.

JUST FOR TODAY, I SHALL RESPECT THE RIGHTS OF ALL LIFE FORMS

All that composes planet earth - water, air, flora, fauna, soil, people, human creations - all these are the creation of God. Humankind does not create except through the inspiration of God, yet we have taken it upon ourselves to become unconscious of God's Divine Plan of Harmony.

It is at this point in the progression of humanity that each and every individual must no longer stand for separatism. We are collective energy from a single Source and when we show disrespect towards ourselves, we harm others, we harm the planet and become unaware of the natural harmony placed here through the creative forces of God.

Humankind has been given all that is needed to live in harmony, respect, love, and oneness. Yet, until we learn to love ourselves, we cannot expect to be in harmony and keeping with God's Divine Plan for the planet. Our space-age technology provides us with new and creative means to link with our neighbors; we share in modern ways of life, thought, and understanding. Yet, most of the world has not yet learned to "take time to smell the flowers." Most of humankind is not connected harmoniously and lovingly to Mother Earth, otherwise we would not treat it with such destructive brutality.

Mother Earth is a living, breathing creation of God. She is linked to humankind as humankind is linked to Earth. We cannot deface her nor our fellow humans without suffering the consequences of our unconscious actions. So, let us become aware of the needs of Mother Earth and the needs of humankind through respect and love. In our growth and awareness let us adopt gentleness, kindness, and consideration for all of God's Creations.

Respect for life is respect for the Divine Wisdom and Love inherent in all creations from the God-Force. All forms of matter radiate sound and light. Our goal is to become aware of the fact that all creations are of the same essence. God has issued from His eternal source of Light a link between all living creatures, "human" or "nonhuman," "physical" or "nonphysical," "intelligent" or without "intelligence," containing a "soul" or not housing a "soul." These terms inadequately try to define what people see with physical eyes and scientific measuring devices. It is of no real significance whether or not humankind places values on the scale of evolution. We are all of, and from, the same source - the God-Force. We are Light.

It is from Light that harmony is made manifest on a constant continuum. It is when humankind rises from the lower human personality and taps the higher spiritual Self, that understanding of the exoteric interrelationship in the sea of esoteric vastness begins. It is when this boundary is broken that the consciousness brings down into the heart the illumination of the Light. Then the Love Consciousness of Christ begins to emanate. It awakens the Love Center. When love flows from the Heart, to Self and others universally, humankind begins to respect the right of all life forms: the planet earth, the water, the trees, the air, the animals and other humans.

THE TWO PRECEPTS OF Reiki Plus®

The First Precept: The Healee must **ask** for healing.

We must "ask" to be healed, and in "asking" open ourselves at the throat level. We vocalize and hear ourself say, "I want to change where I am; I want to change my state of existence." In asking, we are putting forth a conscious decision to become involved. The healee is really the healer. The "healer" is only a channel through which the energy of Reiki flows.

The Second Precept: An equal exchange for service rendered.

There must be an exchange of energy for services, not for the healing. The healing energy belongs to the Universe, to God. However, there needs to be a creative exchange from the recipient, the healee, to the person whose time and services are being offered for balancing and healing. Energy exchange can be anything from the stored form of

energy that we call money, to an exchange of services between the healee and healer. Often we heal loved ones and our own family members. Any time there is an exchange taking place, where one is doing for another consistently, then energy is being exchanged.

Reiki Practitioners offering healing services on a professional level establish fees. The fees set a value on the service, which is considered a concrete reality in the thinking of humankind. Wellness, likewise, has a value, and ultimately reflects the feeling of worthiness and self-love of the people seeking to change their state of health.

Reiki Plus® embraces the Five Spiritual Principles and the Two Precepts of healing,because they are in accord with the Laws of the Universe. If they are fully applied, then a complete healing of the Mind, Body and Emotions will occur. They require the person seeking help to take responsibility for his or her own life.

Remember, we are individuals and we are connected to the Source. We are Battery Chargers and alternator repair persons, who provide a service for those who have lost their connection with the Divine Flow of God's Healing Love. Your time has an exchange value. To violate this-time proven principle of exchange ultimately results in incomplete or ineffective healings.

Compassion and unconditional love hold the individual (the healee) in a state of perfection. The degree of responsibility the healee takes determines the state of wellness he will achieve. Do not allow the healee to be irresponsible, or you have violated an essential precept of **Reiki Plus®** Natural Healing.

Sympathy, on the other hand, holds the individual in the state of Imperfection in which he holds himself. So be clear with your motives. If you desire to see God's Divine healing flow through you with the Reiki, then be true to the time-proven principles of **Reiki Plus®**.

Bring the healee into the consciousness where he will see that his role is to be a part of the healing process, that you alone are not the healer, but that he, the Healee, is the ultimate Healer. His willingness to surrender his fear and become "worthy to receive God's many Blessings" provides the avenue.

THE INITIATIONS

Initiations are required to link one to the Reiki energy. There are four initiations for permanent attunement of the upper chakras. Your Initiations into the vibrations of **Reiki Plus®** are different than Initiations given by Reiki Masters of other Reiki Systems. Your Initiations are a combination of the Ascended Reiki Masters' energy and that of selected Ascended Masters of the Brotherhood of Light, all of whom work only in the Divine Christ Light of the Father.

The specific details surrounding the Initiations given by Masters of **Reiki Plus®**are not revealed publicly. A Master of the **Reiki Plus®** system of Natural Healing is entrusted to withhold this mystical information, as it is likened

18

by us unto the Holy and Mystical Rites of the Sacrament, and is given to the Initiate only after completing his Initiation to Mastership.

The First Initiation attunes both heart chakras: the physical heart (the Fourth Chakra), and the etheric heart (the Eighth Chakra).

The Second Initiation is for the Throat (the Fifth Chakra). It opens the pathway to the higher consciousness centers. The throat and the thyroid gland are the mental body. The Third Initiation is for the Third Eye (the Sixth Chakra), the pituitary gland - the center of higher consciousness.

The Fourth Initiation is for the Crown Chakra (the Seventh Chakra), the pineal gland; it is an attunement to the Spiritual vibration of the Christ-Consciousness center.

Once attuned to the Reiki Ray, the individual can never lose it. However, its energy can be blocked by an individual who rejects his Godself. Reiki cannot be lost, it cannot be given away, and it can only be Initiated by a teacher who has been trained and Initiated with the symbols of power that Dr. Usui himself was given.

On a lighter note, a young man at the age of 9 said, when his mother asked, "Why do you wish to be Initiated into Reiki?" ... "because having the Initiations is like having God take the blocks out of my fingers, so His energy can flow through more fully...."

THE THREE DEGREES OF Reiki Plus® INITIATIONS

There are Three Degrees and Four Levels in the **Reiki Plus®** Natural Healing System. Each activates a particular and unique radiation of energy to be used for a specific purpose in healing or Teaching.

Each Level of Initiation takes the student into a transformation of consciousness, challenging him to grow and stretch his yearning spiritual vision, to experience a more clarifying introspection, to increase his expanding spiral of consciousness.

FIRST DEGREE: Level One

This degree is a permanent attunement to the Reiki Ray. Once Initiated, it allows a person to channel the Reiki for healing himself and others. It requires no special invocation or alteration of the thinking process to "turn on" the flow of the Reiki. By simply placing hands on and opening the heart to love, one automatically brings in the energy.

The First Degree is the foundation of all Three Degrees and must first be mastered thoroughly before one can be considered ready for the next degree. The author usually requires that a student actively utilize the First Degree for at least three months and often longer, before he may continue to the next Degree, for to move too quickly from First to Second does not allow a person a full comprehension of or feeling for the differences of the energy levels. It is necessary to wait until intellectual comprehension begins to be integrated into the sentient understanding of the hands, for the mind and hands to become consciously attuned to and aware of the sensations of what they are thinking and feeling on the body they are touching.

SECOND DEGREE: Level Two

The Second Degree requires further Initiations for attunement to the power Keys utilized in this level. The student is trained to use appropriate Second Degree Keys which provide an increase of power from the Reiki Ray. This degree includes techniques for Absentia (distant healing) and Mental-emotional healing.

In the Second Degree of the **Reiki Plus®** system, the student is further trained in a technique for tapping the collective unconsciousness of the healee. The **Psycho-Therapeutic Reiki**sm Healing modality is a unique process enabling the healer to open the healee to a level where his or her awareness can effect a transmutation of Karma. The effective healing ability of the Practitioner is enhanced to a far greater extent than can be described in this paragraph.

THIRD DEGREE: Level Three - Third Degree Practitioner

Since December 1985, the Third Degree Initiation has been divided into two Levels. Originally it was kept as the Level for Mastership; however, dividing it allows a Practitioner wanting to increase in his healing power to channel the Practitioner's Level of the Third Degree *Reiki Plus* energy. This Level of Energy is not the same Level as that of *Reiki Plus* Mastership; however, the Third Degree Practitioner's Initiation is extremely powerful. It takes the individual to another level of consciousness. Practitioners are encouraged to pursue the Professional Practitioner Certification Program.

Level Four: *Reiki Plus* Mastership

This Degree designates the level of Reiki Mastership, and an authorized Teacher of the *Reiki Plus* System of Natural Healing, with the potential of being invited to become a Faculty member of the *Reiki Plus* Institute.

As directed by the Reiki Masters in Spirit, the author's policy for training potential students to this Level of Initiation is as follows: The student must be so aligned with the *Reiki Plus* Natural Healing system that there is no question in David's Heart, Mind and Spirit that the student's soul purpose and destiny is to be a Reiki Master for life.

The Master's Candidate must be in the completion stage of the *Reiki Plus* Institute's 500 hour Professional Practitioners Program and be a Minister in the Pyramids of Light Church. To reach Mastership, the Candidate must successfully pass all aspects of this comprehensive training. The Candidate's program is tutorial in nature; he travels with the Teacher, at his own expense, to not less than five (5) Reiki First and Second Degree Classes. He is required to write a teaching guideline detailing his understanding of all the comprehensive training learned about *Reiki Plus* Natural Healing. He will assist in the teaching of all phases of the class material and practices. He will also be required to sponsor at least three classes of Reiki to understand this aspect of being a Teacher.

Upon completion of this training the Candidate will be Initiated by David G. Jarrell, the *only* Initiating Master of *Reiki Plus* to legally certify a Reiki Master to teach *Reiki Plus*. Adherence to the provisions contained within the Master-Candidates Contract setforth the requirements to support the objectives and developing students for the *RPI* and coordinating the *RPI* faculty to their center to provide his students the Professional Practitioner's Certification.

THE TWENTY-ONE DAYS OF INITIATION

The twenty-one days of Initiation comprise three cycles through the chakras on each of the three levels of the Heart. This has been thoroughly described in the Chapter "I-Thy-Divine", a progression along the life-long spiral through the Rays in relationship to the Heart levels. This section will shed light on a different perspective, how we are triggered to address growth in a more powerful way.

We know that we enter each level of Initiation into Reiki energy at the Heart Chakra; and that each of the daily initiations of Reiki takes us from the Fourth Chakra up to the Eighth Chakra. However, this is only a small part of the process, as there lies ahead a total balancing of the chakras by the *Reiki Plus* energy.

First, the chakras counterbalance one another during the twenty-one days from the date and time of the first initiation. This means that each day is counted from the time of day you were first initiated. While this counterbalancing is taking place, there is also another overlapping energy refinement taking place, the cycle of the three levels of the Heart.

When the initiations begin the process of balancing the energy levels of the body, there is the balancing of the

20

emotions and spiritual awareness. What can then be expected is a total and in-depth process of seeing, feeling, and projecting of yourself after you have begun your entrance into **Reiki Plus**®. What and how you may have thought before you began **Reiki Plus**® will begin to alter, for Reiki provides an avenue for the expansion of consciousness. The degree of expansion is totally dependent upon your use of **Reiki Plus**® in all areas of your life. **Reiki Plus**® is not limited to the application of healing the body; it serves to stimulate your creativity on all levels: music, art, writing, parenting, clarity of thinking, seeing, hearing and integrating these senses into your more refined faculties.

Now, while the chakras are counterbalancing each other, another important function is taking place; the upper chakras are attuning the corresponding lower chakras to a higher and more refined vibration. This provides a new harmonic resonance to begin opening you to higher octaves of expression. It is a unifying of the chakras.

The spiral up the chakras is directly aligned with the I-Thy-Divine, however, it is only for twenty-one days. In that this is a short cycle, you will remain in each chakra for twenty-four hours and then move up to the next one. The Root Chakra is the beginning point of each cycle, and the Crown Chakra is the concluding point. Each cycle is repeated three times in a row, each cycle uniquely working at each Heart level.

The three cycles through the chakras provide an in-depth look at each state where you are functioning, and begin a cleansing of undesired attitudes, feelings, and concepts. Each step is unique to each person, as you are presently passing through a particular stage of growth when you enter into the **Reiki Plus**® Initiations.

What you will find is the opportunity to see more clearly the self-created obstacles in your life. It is, of course, your choice whether to alter the old patterns of behavior or to remain in them. Obviously remaining in the same patterns will not allow any expansion of your consciousness.

Your approach to the twenty-one day cycle of initiation is entirely up to you. What your reward will be depends on your effort and willingness to open your Heart, to fly into the flames of initiation and to be brave enough to face the void of challenge. The Phoenix awaits you, and only you can begin the flight and see it to its completion.

THE TWENTY-ONE DAY HEALING CYCLE

The twenty-one day healing cycle is likened to the twenty-one days of Initiation. When you begin treatment on another person, he or she begins a cleansing pattern to bring the mind-body-spirit into balance. This cycle needs to be brought to the conscious awareness of the healee. By doing so, he will better understand the reasoning of the up-and-down cycle of his emotions and physical body.

In turn, it provides you with a bench mark to follow the process of the balancing and the trials that are concretely factual within the framework of the healee's personality and physiological challenges. When you apply this to the "Healing Curve" that is discussed more thoroughly later in its own chapter (see Chapter 5) and during the class, you will see the importance of treating the healee (client) three days in a row and then as deemed needed according to the responses and reactions of the healee to the healing process.

The importance of your awareness of this natural healing process can not be over stressed. Since you, in the healer's role, will be called upon by the healee to provide positive input to the "whys and wherefores of the healing experiences", you will need to be observant of the healee's apparent state of imbalance before starting the healing sessions. Training in this area comes from proper training and the trust that God will not present you with someone you are unable to help. There may be times when your trust level is challenged. This is how God teaches us trust and the knowing that He and the Healee are the true healers.

Chapter Two

HEALING AND THE LAW

The laws of the United States allow healing (touching the body of another person) to be performed by licensed physicians, nurses, and massage therapist. Healing performed by those who are not in these categories must be ministers of a church in which healing by touch or subtle energy is a part of the church's official function.

If you want to do healing on a professional level and to receive a fee or donation for your services, then it is wise to become ordained in a recognized church of healing. Be sure that you investigate the church and learn about its tenets and philosophies; this is the only way that you will know if you are in agreement with the church's basic objectives. Associating yourself with a church allows you to be actively involved with its functions and purposes. The use of healing through touch must be specifically stated in the Articles of Incorporation.

The Pyramids of Light, Inc., a Church of Natural Healing, under the directorship of David G. Jarrell, is a non-denominational Christ-Conscious church. Its spiritual philosophy is based on the Laws of the Universe, the teachings of the "Christed Ones" and the Ascended Masters. It holds no Doctrines and Creeds allowing the individual to seek God in all of God's creation. Ministers of the church come from varied philosophical and theological backgrounds. The Pyramids of Light, Inc. is not a religious organization in the typical sense. Our purpose is to provide a vehicle for groups and individuals to join in meditation and to share **Reiki Plus**® healing.

Students of **Reiki Plus**® interested in this Ministry may write for an Application to: Pyramids of Light, Inc., for address see back of the book. Applicants must have completed **Reiki Plus**® First Degree and have used Reiki daily for self healing for at least six months. This application will provide additional information concerning the requirements for Ordination and the responsibilities and obligations of an Associate Minister. All Ministers are first Ordained as Associate Ministers. Full Ministerial status may be attained upon completion of Ministerial training.

Pyramids of Light, Inc., a church of healing, is recognized under the codes of the I.R.S. of the United States of America as a Private Foundation (subtitled Church) and is duly given the status of 501(c)(3), 509(a)(1). This is a "non-profit" status. Our state of Incorporation is California and our date April 22, 1983. Our Ministers are provided the rights and privileges of Ministers in accordance with the laws of the various states and counties in which they perform their functions as Ministers and by their level of ordination in the Pyramids of Light, Inc., by its Senior Minister and the Board of Directors.

GUIDELINE OF CONTRACT FOR HEALING

The following outline shall serve as an official guideline for all **Reiki Plus**® students . Comprehensive material is presented to students who go beyond the level of First Degree **Reiki Plus**®. The guideline is used to establish the Legal and Ethical relationship between the student/practitioner and the client requesting his or her services. The beginning relationship is established by verbal or written agreement. However, this contract must be clearly understood, accepted, and completed prior to the beginning of the healing process, that is, the series of treatments necessary to reach the stated goal of wellness desired in life.

The following items are to be adhered to by all **Reiki Plus**® students/practitioners:

1. **Reiki Plus**® and **PSEB**^{sm} are empirical in their approach, treating the whole person, not merely the symptoms. Empiricism is defined as "observation, or practical experience apart from scientific knowledge."

2. Natural Healers may not, without being in violation of the law, treat a pathological disease, i.e., you cannot treat pneumonia; however, you can treat a client for difficulty in breathing or congestion.

3. The healee (client) must make a verbal acknowledgement stating his or her responsibility in creating the imbalance and a commitment to participate in the healing process.

4. The healee must agree to make an exchange (of energy) in some form with the healer for his services.

5. You and the healee must agree to treat the _entire_ _body_, not just the specific areas. Balance will not be returned to the body by partial treatments.

6. The healee must agree to communicate to you when his desired level of energy has been reached - where his energy is balanced and is recreating a state of well-being.

7. The healee is to be advised that the speed of healing and the number of treatments are totally dependent upon his participation. If treatments are stopped before the mind-body-spirit is at-one-ment, the potential regeneration of the body and its vital energy will not be reached.

8. You, as a Reiki channel, can make no promises whatever of curing, miracles or other such considerations. Explain only that the healing system being used is designed to balance the vital energy. This allows the healee to deal with the existing spiritual separation between his physical body, mental perception and his higher self. This realization begins the process of healing. The healee is responsible for repairing the fragmentation that exists between his personality (ego) fears and his potential God-Self. The Healer has the responsibility to do all that he can to encourage the healee to seek and attain his God-given Right - spiritual wholeness, from this physical, mental and emotional holism follows.

9. A natural healer, _unless_ _licensed_, you cannot prescribe foods, drugs, vitamins, minerals, herbs or any combination thereof without violating the law, nor can you ever suggest that the client stop taking a prescribed medication.

10. You must know when a person should be treated by a medical specialist, either concurrently with natural healing or independently by the physician, chiropractor or other medical doctor needed by the client. Please do not ever allow your ego to prevent you from acknowledging the need of all approaches to healing. There are times when a client must have medical assistance and you would be legally and morally wrong to advise him otherwise.

11. Know that your true purpose as a channel for the Reiki Ray is to be without expectations. That you hold the person in the state of perfection which will assist his achieving the desired state of wellness.

23

Chapter Three

THE CHAKRAS

The Chakras corresponding glands and organs

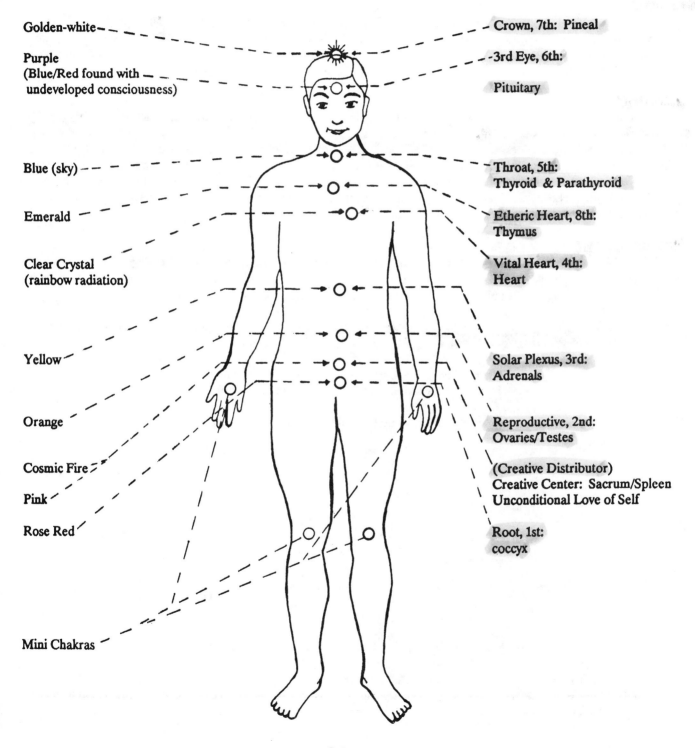

Golden-white

Purple
(Blue/Red found with
undeveloped consciousness)

Blue (sky)

Emerald

Clear Crystal
(rainbow radiation)

Yellow

Orange

Cosmic Fire

Pink

Rose Red

Mini Chakras

Crown, 7th: Pineal

3rd Eye, 6th:

Pituitary

Throat, 5th:
Thyroid & Parathyroid

Etheric Heart, 8th:
Thymus

Vital Heart, 4th:
Heart

Solar Plexus, 3rd:
Adrenals

Reproductive, 2nd:
Ovaries/Testes

(Creative Distributor)
Creative Center: Sacrum/Spleen
Unconditional Love of Self

Root, 1st:
coccyx

CHAKRAS

Crown, 7th:

Spiritual Life force: Pineal gland, the Christ Conscious Center. Cosmic Fire from God flows through the 6th etheric body (the Eighth Chakra) into the Lotus at the crown. When opened, provides stimulation of the pineal hormone production: melatonin. This is the center where Higher conscious desire begins for the Aspirant. It is where illusion must evolve through the Trials of Fire to reach Illumination. The Light of the Cosmic Fire provides the light to be refracted through the cells of the body and into the Third Eye for the evolvement of Spiritual Sight.

3rd Eye, 6th:

Higher Consciousness, emotional and spiritual love center; spiritual inner sight, clairvoyance. Pituitary gland. When balanced, the mind (right hemisphere) and brain (left hemisphere) function in a unified field. Insight ensues and its practical application becomes a daily occurrence. When opened for spiritual growth the personality consciousness slowly dissolves as the illusion of duality unifies in the **trinity of oneness: I AM Illumination.**

Throat, 5th:

Outer communication and the beginning of inner hearing; clairaudience. Life and breath center; thyroid and parathyroid glands; mental functions. The 5th chakra is the gateway to the Higher Consciousness and the gateway through which the emotions contained in the heart must pass to become balanced and harmonized. When the Throat Chakra is consciously opened, the process of refinement is continuous, for we exist in levels within levels. Each awareness contributes its own kind of awareness, a pyramidal progress towards full consciousness. This center is always a participant in all psycho-physical imbalances. A person must willingly change his mental concepts to recognize the old through the habits that have been holding him in a state of imbalance.

Etheric Heart, 8th:

Co-creative God consciousness, the acceptance of the God within. Thymus. Ray of Truth. When we awaken the 8th chakra, wellness is an integral part of our path. Life takes on the happiness and joy of Love which pours forth from the eternal blessings of our united presence with God. We can utilize the power of the God-Force.

The Thymus gland controls the immune system and is fully functional when the physical body (chakras, glands and organs) utilizes the thymus' governing imprint. The double pyramid connection is:

Thyroid-Liver-Spleen and Adrenal-Liver-Spleen, where
the Thymus is a vertical or superimposed pyramid point of these.

Upper Pyramidal Mental (Female/Mind) Consciousness

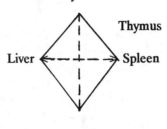

Male (Right Side) or Yang
Acid Based

Female (Left Side) or Yin
Alkaline Based

Lower Pyramidal Ego Survival/Reactive (Male/Brain) Consciousness

For God to flow into us the personality must be seeking Illumination through the "in - breath" of the Cosmic Fire (the Golden - White Light of the Christ Consciousness). This will unify the 6th chakra, the Pituitary. Then, as the male (brain) and female (mind) are no longer antagonistic, proper hormone balance will be established.

This functional balance can be looked at from another perspective, that of the psycho-physical components within the male/female aspects of oneself and glandular/organ activity:

Male: Thymus-Pineal-Hypothalamus-Posterior Lobe Pituitary-Right Lobe-Thyroid/Parathyroid - Liver/Spleen (lower pyramidal ego consciousness) -Right Adrenal - Pancreas - Testes (Prostate) - Sacrum - coccyx.

Female: Thymus-Pineal-Hypothalmus-Anterior Lobe Pituitary-Left Lobe Thyroid/Parathyroid - Liver/Spleen (Upper Pyramidal Mental consciousness) Left Adrenal - Pancreas - Ovaries - Sacrum - Coccyx.

Vital Heart, 4th:

The center hub, where all emotions are recorded. The diamond fire of the Christ Consciousness, the "I AM Presence," must rise above the ego consciousness to reach the God-Consciousness of the 8th chakra. Then one can heal the mind, body and emotions through the process of illumination; passing upward into the levels within levels: the refinement of consciousness into spiritual awareness. The body-mind will follow either by being totally healed or by acknowledging its karmic need of the existing genetic potential, where the individual learns to live in a blessed state of acceptance. Healing is not always physical.

Solar Plexus, 3rd:

Where mental control must be gained over the desire body. When this energy is focused, we can clearly direct the power of the 1st and 2nd chakras and manifest the "Love-Will-Wisdom." At this point wisdom has transcended desire and our higher self will evolve in the physical-mental conscious state of existence. The creative Intellect is expressed in our everyday existence. This figurative transcendence is understood at the completion of the **8th Ray**, where the male/female bridges "intellectual duality", the separatism that existed between the two selves and the power directing the ego. The Eight Ray evolvement brings about the inner marriage, where " ...when two are gathered together, I AM Present...." and the Creative Mind embraces the Wisdom of Christ Consciousness and lives with God's Divine Will prevailing over the human consciousness.

Sexual Center, 2nd:

Sexual urges of the body. This center is the procreative center of the body and is directed by the reproductive organs. The glandular correspondence are ovaries (women) and testes (men). On the physical plane these Centers provide the pathways through which our spiritual co-creative powers take physical form. God's way of sharing the experience of the ever-continuing process of life everlasting

Root, 1st:

Known as the kundalini or serpent's fire; life force for survival. If undisciplined: fear, fight and flight; if disciplined: secure understanding of the endless source of power from the infinite Spirit of which we are an integral part in Oneness. The root chakra's expression of energy is directly related to a person's quality of health. The **cosmic fire** that awaits release lies dormant, until the higher self can properly utilize the potency of its ethereal energy source on physical and spiritual levels of life.

The Root Chakra is fed by the "Cosmic Fire" from the God Source. For this to occur, the 8th and 7th Chakras must be mentally and physically awakened through chakra meditation or meditative Yoga. This will allow spiritual consciousness to manifest integration within all of the individual's cells.

The Cosmic Fire must be actively breathed down the central core of the spine to fuel the Root Chakra. By doing so the individual begins the expansion of the physical body and the desire of the mental body to clear out the old patterns that have been restrictive to his spiritual growth. When an individual passes through the 4th Chakra in his Second Passage through the Rays, this energy takes on another dynamic. The individual moves through the remaining fragments of the "Living to Die Consciousness." He then begins his outward journey beyond his "old shell" to realize a "Living to Heal Consciousness." This has been named by the author as the expansion of the "Consciousness Bubble", the multi dimensional expansion of the ego beyond the "Old Limitations" once considered to be problems and now realized as opportunities and challenges to reach the God Self.

SYMBOLS OF CHAKRA ENCRYPTION

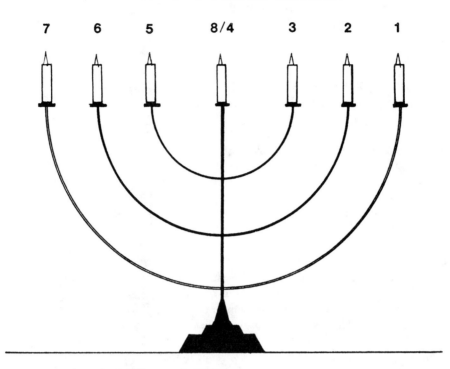

7 6 5 8/4 3 2 1

The Hermetic Axiom, "So as above, so as below." This axiom is shown in the symbolism of the ceremonial candelabrum. Each chakra is counterbalanced by one above and one below the 4th/8th Heart Chakra. Therefore, the chakras relate to each other thus:

7 is to 1
6 is to 2
5 is to 3
8 is to 4

PYRAMIDAL CHAKRA RELATIONSHIPS

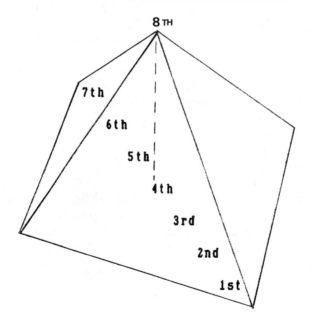

8th Chakra, Thymus, the Outer shell of Trust (trusting our Inner God Self)

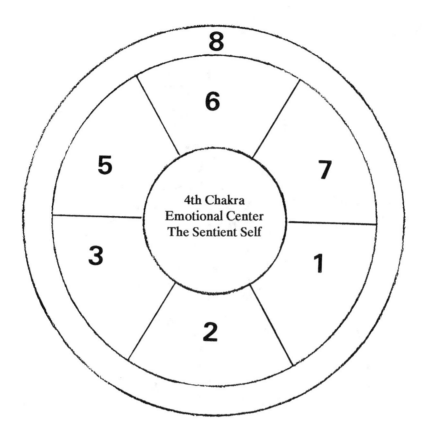

Creative Sacral Distributor

This is a complex center composed of 8 parts, one for each chakra. It is the center which allows either the full or the partial flow of the Cosmic Fire from the Kundalini (coccyx), the Root Chakra. Partial flow is directly related to the conflicted consciousness of the individual. The chakra centers receiving restricted energy distribution therefore display the feelings of violation of their Sacred self. The feelings of "sin and guilt" are blocking the distribution due to the individual's inability to accept the forgiveness God has already given; therefore, being unable to forgive himself and the other person, he feels and/or thinks violated him and thanking the person for sharing in your growth and understanding.

The distribution of light into the physical body from the chakra bodies controlling the glands and organs respondent to the chakras is directly related to how an individual handles the challenges of life. The connection of the Cosmic Fire in the coccyx to the "C/P Point" (glands penis or clitoris) of the individual and up the front of the center line of the body to the pineal gland defines how issues of life are dealt with day to day. A disconnection between the coccyx and the C/P Point indicate that issues are put behind the individual and in time distorts the spine. Spinal imbalance creates interference in the flow of life energy through the peripheral nerves to the organs and tissue of the body.

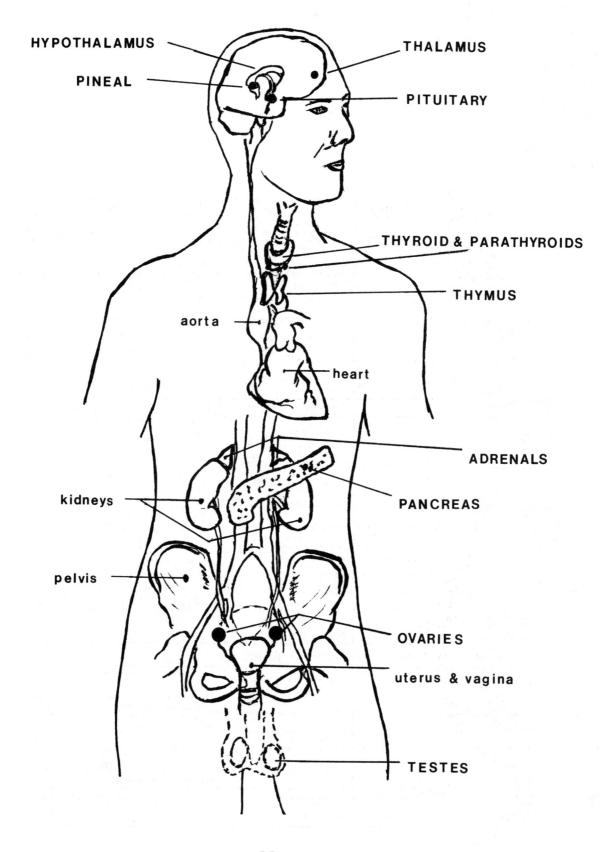

CHART OF EFFECTS OF SPINAL MISALIGNMENTS

Chakras to spinal vertebrae:

7th Occiput Protuberance Bump
6th Atlas (C1)
5th C5 - C7
8th T2
4th T2 - T4
3rd T9
2nd L3
CDC Sacrum
1st coccyx

ATLAS
AXIS
CERVICAL SPINE
1st THORACIC
THORACIC SPINE
1st LUMBAR
LUMBAR SPINE
SACRUM
COCCYX

Vertebrae	Areas	Effects
1C	Blood supply to the head, pituitary gland, scalp, bones of the face, brain, inner and middle ear, sympathetic nervous system.	Headaches, nervousness, insomnia, head colds, high blood pressure, migraine headaches, nervous breakdowns, amnesia, chronic tiredness, dizziness.
2C	Eyes, optic nerves, auditory nerves, sinuses, mastoid bones, tongue, forehead.	Sinus trouble, allergies, crossed eyes, deafness, eye troubles, earache, fainting spells, certain cases of blindness.
3C	Cheeks, outer ear, face bones, teeth, trifacial nerve.	Neuralgia, neuritis, acne or pimples, eczema.
4C	Nose, lips, mouth, eustachian tube.	Hay fever, catarrh, hearing loss, adenoids.
5C	Vocal cords, neck glands, pharynx.	Laryngitis, hoarseness, throat conditions such as sore throat or quinsy.
6C	Neck muscles, shoulders, tonsils.	Stiff neck, pain in upper arm, tonsillitis, whooping cough, croup.
7C	Thyroid gland, bursae in the shoulders, elbows.	Bursitis, colds, thyroid conditions.
1T	Arms from the elbows down, including hands, wrists, and fingers; esophagus and trachea.	Asthma, cough, difficult breathing, shortness of breath, pain in lower arms and hands.
2T	Heart, including its valves and covering; coronary arteries.	Functional heart conditions and certain chest conditions.
3T	Lungs, bronchial tubes, pleura, chest, breast.	Bronchitis, pleurisy, pneumonia, congestion, influenza.
4T	Gall bladder, common duct.	Gall bladder conditions, jaundice, shingles.
5T	Liver, solar plexus, blood.	Liver conditions; fevers, low blood pressure, anemia, poor circulation, arthritis.
6T	Stomach.	Stomach troubles, including nervous stomach, indigestion, heartburn, dyspepsia.
7T	Pancreas, duodenum.	Ulcers, gastritis.
8T	Spleen	Lowered resistance.
9T	Adrenal and supra-renal glands.	Allergies, hives.
10T	Kidneys.	Kidney troubles, hardening of the arteries, chronic tiredness, nephritis, pyelitis.
11T	Kidneys, ureters.	Skin conditions such as acne, pimples, eczema, or boils.
12T	Small intestines, lymph circulation.	Rheumatism, gas pains, certain types of sterility.
1L	Large intestines, inguinal rings.	Constipation, colitis, dysentery, diarrhea, some ruptures or hernias.
2L	Appendix, abdomen, upper leg.	Cramps, difficult breathing, acidosis, varicose veins.
3L	Sex organs, uterus, bladder, knees.	Bladder troubles, menstrual troubles such as painful or irregular periods, miscarriages, bed wetting, impotency, change of life symptoms, many knee pains.
4L	Prostate gland, muscles of the lower back, sciatic nerve.	Sciatica; lumbago; difficult, painful, or too frequent urination; backaches.
5L	Lower legs, ankles, feet.	Poor circulation in the legs, swollen ankles, weak ankles and arches, cold feet, weakness in the legs, leg cramps.
SACRUM	Hip bones, buttocks.	Sacro-iliac conditions, spinal curvatures.
COCCYX	Rectum, anus.	Hemorrhoids (piles), pruritis (itching), pain at end of spine on sitting.

Region labels: NECK REGION (1C–7C), MID-BACK (1T–12T), LOW BACK (1L–5L), PELVIS (Sacrum, Coccyx)

© Parker Chiropractic Research Foundation, 1975
Litho in U.S.A.

Chapter Four

UNDERSTANDING HOW DISEASE AND HEALING MANIFESTS

"Pandora's Box" and the "Tumbleweed Theory" of Health

It is important for us to be aware that every experience we have is chosen, consciously or unconsciously, as a tool for growth. We are often unaware that our actions and thoughts create barriers that must be correctly and constructively understood; our actions reflect our choices which lead to balance or imbalance.

Our understanding of truth is directly proportional to our willingness to admit to ourselves that we are responsible for the day-to-day occurrences presented to us. Often we choose to not deal with emotional situations as they present themselves. Instead we choose to place the "things-to-do-tomorrow" in "Pandora's Box." When we place into "Pandora's Box" that which we are not willing to confront, we accumulate stress that must be confronted at a later time. These individual steps are like the building blocks of a wall. If we continually allow this illusion in our interplay with people, responsibilities and decisions, we will continue to create and compound complex misdirected emotions.

The Tumbleweed Theory describes the process of accumulating stress. Each time we choose not to confront an opportunity (a stress situation) and learn the particular lesson we need to learn, we add to our energy imbalance. Each imbalance is seen as a "tic-mark" on the blackboard of our Aura. When the "tic-marks" outweigh the positive life force energy (reflected in emotional spiritual and physical well-being) then we begin to wobble off center. So begins the life spiral into unwellness, the Self-rejection symbolized by the "thoughtform" we chose as our teacher. Let us look at how we allow such an unnecessary "thought-form" to fester into disease.

When we do not allow ourselves to deal with opportunities for growth, we begin clogging up the "passageways of communication." If we continue to feed into "Pandora's Box," then we begin blocking the functional balance of our lives. Imbalances (accumulated trauma) eventually become states of unwellness. The areas of the body that become "unwell" correspond to and reflect the inner states of emotion in which learning was not completed. All functions are a part of the sum. There is no separation of above and below (spirit and flesh) in the body or in consciousness. We must deal with all aspects of our lives. So, what we must do is realize that the flow, balance and harmony, come from above as well as from within.

We must be willing to open our throat center, the 5th chakra, to speak and hear the truth of the Heart, to go beyond our fear of rejection. This fear is a sub-element of the Fear of Non-Approval which is the foundation of incomplete Love: "conditional love." This is where the individual begins to actualize separation in his personal and social behavioral patterns.

Feelings of insecurity are founded upon separation from God. Biblical history reflects this at the time of Adam. Adam was removed from the Garden of Eden, and as he became aware of his body and carnal life he began to take on denser forms of feeling. Humankind began to feel that God created conditional love as punishment for Adam. Interestingly enough, humans created conditional love, for God does not hold us in guilt or in sin; we hold ourselves in these states. So, the enlightenment comes with the realization that we impose our own limitations, barriers, and blockages. We separate ourselves from the God-self which lies within the Heart of everyone.

We are under the illusion that we must please those with whom we are involved; sometimes at all costs, even if it means being untruthful. Fortunately, this is not necessarily so. What we are dealing with, when we feel we need to please others, is conditional love. We fear that if we express our emotions truthfully, we may lose that which we have created (sometimes falsely) in a relationship.

To reach the awareness that we are worthy of Love, we must first accept our worthiness to receive. One of the Reiki principles says: "Just for today I shall accept my many blessings." This means allowing our conscious self to open up to the higher Christ-Consciousness within and to accept the blessings from God. Humankind has forgotten that every person is an eternal spark from God. God's Love and abundance are provided unconditionally to all, so that we may, in return, unconditionally share the Divine energy of life.

For eons humankind has rationalized guilt, rather than accept the Love that God has to offer. All of the lessons that are presented to us ultimately bring us closer to God. Lessons are opportunities, not problems, blockages, or limitations. We choose, consciously or unconsciously, each lesson by exercising or not exercising free will.

One of the first things that must be fully accepted is that we are worthy of love and that we are a part of God. In doing so, we build the first important foundation that allows us to accept all that God offers in return for the effort that we put forth. This means do not judge yourself by another's standards. If our effort is honest, "if we earn our living honestly," then we shall receive abundance and fulfill all levels of our human and spiritual aspirations.

People sometimes feel that they have the right to judge others. Our judgments have been and will continue to be a force blocking our growth into higher states of Light. It is Grace, the integrity with which we put forth our effort, that is most important.

We must learn to understand and live the two Great Laws and Commandments: To Love the Lord thy God, with all thy Heart, with all thy Soul, and with all thy Mind; and the second: To love thy neighbor as thyself. Until we are able to love ourselves, we can love no other. The divinity and the trinity of Mind, Body, and Spirit are the triangulation of bringing humankind, God, and the Christ-Light "within" into balance. When we love ourselves as our neighbor, then we are conscious that we and our neighbor are equals. All we do to ourselves, we likewise do unto our neighbor. Our neighbor is not only the person next door, but all "Creations of Light" who share and inhabit the earth and the solar system, God's Cosmic Infinity.

It is the complex emotional state of holding within the Heart the fears of not being worthy, of being guilty or of possibly blocking our acceptance of Love that lead to unwellness. The Heart is the center and basis of all wellness; to achieve this level of health, we must be open to seeking the truth, the "highest and best" soul purpose offered in our life opportunities. By peeling away the false illusions of the ego self, we allow the simple release of our emotional needs: the immature conditions and expectations of idealistic "love".

We all need to be loved. What we must find in our own Hearts is the presence of God's Love to know true communion with Love. By living this state of Grace, we truly can love ourselves and all of our brothers and sisters, and live together in harmony. It is from harmony that wellness results.

THE PREDISPOSITION TO WELLNESS

The Soul is a continuous energy form which collects, contains and retains all knowledge from the beginning of the Soul's creation. The Soul element has a wisdom far beyond that of the average "intellect" because it carries the infinite wisdom of God's Light to be illumined in the human monad (body) in each incarnation. The Soul's journey from God into human form transcends space and time to manifest spiritual fulfillment, the Reality of God's Truth.

The Mind, our Spiritual link to the Eternal Light, guides the pathway of learning for each incarnation. To embrace our Spiritual connection from the unconscious Mind to the conscious mind activates the rational, intellectual center of the brain. It is at this point of building an all-encompassing vehicle that the Soul enters into conscious action in preparation for those lessons needed for its Spiritual illumination. The process by which we take that action, creating full responsibility for each incarnation, is described in this Chapter. We will see how each of us can no longer look elsewhere to lay blame for our lack of health, unhappiness or any other state of emotional or Spiritual disparity.

We are Light, and either we use this unlimited resource for our total well-being or we swim in a fog until somewhere in our soul's journey illumination is accepted. Let us continue now to see how each incarnation allows us to understand our journey through human existence.

First the Soul chooses the parents who will provide the proper genetic characteristics. The socioeconomic and philosophical basis of the family are the factors explicitly needed to project the soul-personality into a conscious union with God. Your Predisposition to Wellness includes the fact that you have chosen, prior to entering the physical body, conditions for your individual Soul's growth. The Soul's intent is very specific; because it knows the challenges the personality has to a chosen family. Each person must confront his chosen trials, so that he may expand to a "Living to Heal Consciousness".

The quality of the parents and friends and the economic and social framework of the family shape the evolving consciousness of the personality - lower Ego, the 3rd Chakra fear center. The learned personality traits are reflected in the character of the individual, uniting the Creative Intellect with the Creative Mind (left-right brain balancing) and expanding the Ego beyond fear. Thus the environmental influences are direct contributing factors to all levels of the unfoldment of the Soul's growth.

The Soul's life situations (usually viewed as "problems") are what afford growth opportunities in a particular lifetime. What is called "stress" or "trauma" is an unbalanced reaction to one's own chosen growth "opportunities." "Opportunities" are the true challenges that provide energy and impetus for the continual unfolding and development of our consciousness.

Free will has been ours from our first moment of Creation. Our free will has never ceased to function and it has never been taken away from anyone. It is the use of free will that directs the course of our life; self-discipline enables us to use it to its optimum capacity. Free will is active in all circumstances, even those situations we see as being imposed on us from the outside. Our Free Will can never be destroyed or nullified by others.

Your free will has chosen for you to be exactly where you are at the present moment in the specific circumstances of your life. Through these circumstances you may elect, or not elect, to learn the lessons in this lifetime that lead to greater balance, harmony, strength and, ultimately, union with God.

From this point of view, we need not look at disease as a negative manifestation, for it is influenced, as all things are, by the Soul's "predisposition." Any pain, stress, upset, disharmony and disease need not be looked upon as something "bad," for they are all great teachers in the lessons we have chosen to learn in this incarnation. Disease is a very loud message from the Higher Self to the lower self; it screams, Listen to me, hear me. I, your Higher Self, have not registered in your conscious Mind, physical Body, and personality." You have gotten in your own way. Disease is another way many people choose to stop and to learn how to listen to the Higher Self. It can, and ultimately must (either in this lifetime or another) provide a greater opportunity for learning about the obstacles we place in front of ourselves and have not wished to confront until this point.

We must deal with life's "opportunities" as they arise, or otherwise they will be forced down into the unconscious mind. As that unused energy collects, it becomes like the mythological symbol of "Pandora's Box." One day, that energy must and will emerge, quite often in the form of physical stress, anger or unwellness. It is very difficult to understand why we have a disease when we do not understand the emotions that have caused this imbalance. What was once put away, shoved down under, must be recognized, dealt with, and released in order for balance to be restored and health maintained.

The key to discovering how the psycho-physical manifestation of disease occurs lies in the closing of the throat region. The throat is what we close when we wish to retain the feelings and emotions that we do not desire to confront. This containment in the throat allows for the buildup of energy to be turned inward and initially manifests as nonproductiveness in the form of misdirected, inharmonious patterns of behavior. Eventually, it may lead to more serious psycho-physical manifestations in the forms of stress and unwellness.

No function (physical, emotional or spiritual) inside the individual can be separated; these functions are all interconnected and interrelated. The endocrine glands play a vital part in the Physio-Spiritual balancing process of the individual.

The endocrine glands are stimulated, from the viewpoint of the medical community, by neurotransmitters. A

33

call is sent through the nerves to the brain to begin stimulating of the glands to release the hormones needed by the body. The endocrine glands are called "ductless" because they do not have special ducts through which the hormones travel to associated glands and organs of the body; rather the hormones are released into the general circulation, the bloodstream.

As explained later in this Chapter in section, "Etheric Energy Patterns of the Chakras," Closing the Throat - The Causal Factor diagram, each outer or subtle body and chakra connects directly to a specific vertebrae nerve, and each nerve connects directly to a specific endocrine gland. The third outer body (the mental body) is specifically linked to the throat; the thyroid/parathyroid center. By closing at the throat center, we not only affect the glands of that center, we also set up a chain-reaction effect that influences all the other important gland/chakra centers.

When we hold within and close down the functions of the throat, we also limit the release of inner emotions held back at this level. We begin to compound the inner emotions because we are not willing to bring them forth from the Heart (and other dysfunctional organs and/or glandular centers) to express them in words. Words describe our feelings; however feelings, come first and we have created words to express our fears, pains, joy and happiness.

On an physical level, closing down the throat center limits mental communication between the Heart, the Body, and our higher state of consciousness. On an etheric level we restrict the receptivity of the first and second etheric bodies by closing down the avenue through which the hormonal supply from the thymus, pineal, pituitary and thyroid/parathyroid glands enter the heart, adrenals, reproductive glands and the kundalini center. (For the location of the endocrine glands, please see the chart in Section 3 under Diagrams.)

This resulting decreased activity of the adrenal glands in turn affects the thyroid/parathyroid functions. This is due to the correspondence that exists between the Third Chakra (adrenals) and the Fifth Chakra (thyroid/parathyroid) i.e., the chakras respond to the Hermetic Law: "As above, so below." (See Chakra correspondence diagram in Chakra Section.) This hormonal restriction of the thyroid/parathyroid/5th Throat Chakra restricts the ability of the body to transform foods, to assimilate calcium, and to produce heat and energy necessary for the body's metabolism. Through this, the many other hormonal and organ functions of the body are reduced. We can see, closing the throat leads to an internal vicious that sets up a self perpetuating pattern of hormonal deficiency, reduced physical stamina and Spiritual deprivation.

The constriction of the throat chakra breaks a link in the chain of a perfectly balanced hormonal system. Through heart-felt communication, we can alter and correct the multitudes of pathologies that humankind has created by improper thought-forms. Illness is the manifestation of an "imperfect" thought form: mind and body are disjointed, restricting Mind from being in direct contact with Soul consciousness. It is necessary to clearly see (identify) one's "Predisposition," to reconnect Personality - Soul consciousness with Spirit. This reestablishes the natural flow and internal harmony that lead to wellness of the mental, emotional body allowing the physical body to then reach its potential state of function.

WELLNESS: WALKING IN MEDITATION

It is not through a process of words, ritualism or intellectual understanding that we find health and Everlasting Life. It is through an active and direct experiential process of attuning to our Spiritual nature. When we are born, we have a close connection to the Spiritual Life, having just left the Spirit realm. We are still **Light** in our essential connection, and in some ways still very fragile. Young children can communicate directly with the angelic kingdom; their communication is the nonverbal telepathic language that is used in that kingdom. Infants can see the surrounding light energy forms (entities) because their Third Eye and higher consciousness are still open. Because of this communication and vision children are able to amuse themselves for long periods of time; laughter are angelic sounds resonating their attunement to subtle energy.

The indoctrination into the values of the world, certain human values arbitrarily deemed "real", slowly pull us away from the God Within, the Spirit and Angelic Kingdom. Through this heavy-handed indoctrination, the pineal gland, once opened like the lotus blossom receiving the Light illuminating higher states of awareness, closes down, limiting its productivity on emotional, spiritual, conscious and hormonal levels. When the pineal closes down, then the thymus hormone (the eighth chakra) linked to the God Center cannot flow down into the body. This gland, as with the others, becomes less productive and less capable of creating and sustaining health.

Western medicine does not yet recognize the tremendous importance these glands play in the overall health of the individual. It has been a standing opinion that the thymus gland atrophies. Only recently, around 1980, it was discovered that the pineal gland produces a hormone called melatonin. Melatonin has, thus far, been found to be an important hormone in controlling and eliminating stress, alcoholism, and the accumulation of low density lipid proteins inside of the body.

Meditation is esoterically known to be an effective way to reduce stress in the system. Meditation is a way of opening up the pineal gland, awakening the lotus and bringing the White Light of the Christ-Consciousness into the physical being. The powerful effects of meditation can now be scientifically explained through the releasing of melatonin into the to act as the anti-stress agent which establishes and maintains balance and peace within.

Radiant health comes through our attunement to the purpose behind this specific incarnation. What has happened to us since birth has all been for one particular reason: to speed our awakening and enlightenment. Disease is merely a loud reminder of how far from God we have drifted. Understand, however, that often the further you feel from God, in reality, the closer you are. In the circle of life, our inner search, the chosen experiences provide opportunity at any moment to awaken us to our Co-Creative God Presence. When this awakening occurs, the illusions disperse and the all-surrounding, all-encompassing Reality of God's Love, Joy and Peace illuminates within our Heart. The circle is completed, we have returned to our source: God. At this magnificent moment we sparkle with radiance. We have run a full circle, looking and finding our reason for being on this planet: Love. Love is Divine Will made manifest in our Heart, as we focus the Christ Conscious "I AM" into the all-encompassing Light of God.

The God within isn't some untouchable being. It isn't something so awesome and spectacular that we should stand in awe of it. God has been with us all of our lives, and God has always been available to His children.

"MY GOD -- TO ME"

My God to me is not some vague, unknown, mystical entity who lives
somewhere in the Great Beyond.

My God to me is my Friend, real and loving and personal who lives
within the Heart and Soul of me.

Judith M. Gomez

Man is made in the Image of God, and God's image can only be perfect. Man's perception of his imperfection is merely a temporary state of "dreaming," of not seeing the Light within, the God Consciousness. Once the "dream" of imperfection has been recognized for what it is, we no longer need to feel frightened of God. In reality, God could never be apart from you, or you would cease to exist. Our improper creations are merely mistakes in perception of who we really are and where we come from. The Christ is alive inside of your Heart, in God's Heart, in all Hearts: It awaits the conscious expression of your **I AM**.

BE WILLING TO SPEAK, BE WILLING TO LISTEN

In God's Reality, there is no separation, there is no judgment. These concepts are a creation of man, or more aptly put, a fearful creation of man. No one is better, higher, lower, more than or less than anybody else. This concept involves being able to see values within values -- to see beyond appearances, beyond judgment, to be able to stand upright in God's Light and be willing to let go of our man-made illusions. Often this may look like an act of giving up our own will or individuality. This thought can be frightening to the "separate" self that furiously guards it's ego.

However, as soon as we understand that this belief always involves pain, stress, fear, anger, loneliness, and disease, we begin to recognize that it may no longer be desirable. Our True-Self, our God-Self, never produces these elements in our lives. The God-Self is in all people, and we have these elements within our lives right now. God's greatest gift to His children is Love: the act of giving and receiving Love. To distinguish between the God-Self and the ego, we need to look at how we feel inside.

Are we peaceful? Are we joyful? Can we give Love in a particular circumstance or do we wish to harbor other thoughts of separation? God has never left us, only the dark clouds of miscreated thought-forms anchored inside of our spiritual bodies temporarily cloud our vision of God's ever-present abundance.

We do not have to go anywhere to find God and our True-Self. He is here now, within; and, it is our choice (for God has given His children the gift of choice) to listen to the voice of Love or the voices of fear and anguish.

God is not unattainable; this is a fallacy that has been perpetuated by many of the organized religions. God is not "out there," God is in the Heart. We must begin, one step at a time: to know and to feel, to recognize our power of choice and take responsibility for choosing. We must Love that person we look at in the mirror each day and learn to become very honest with that person. We must be willing to stop pulling the covers up over our head and shoving our emotions down out of sight.

Faith is required for you to realize and believe that you have all the strength and Love and support in God's Kingdom to fully communicate and carry out all the opportunities you have chosen for yourself in this incarnation. All we have is today. All we ever have is the **ever-present future**. Miracles need but one second to occur. Time is a concept of Man, another of his misperceptions. We have all we need, right now, to be full, alive, well, happy, and at peace. Give yourself the gift of being who you are, right now, for that is the child that God Loves. Give yourself the gift of being willing to speak from your heart and the gift of being able to listen from your heart. It within the heart that **Truth** is found. It is the 8th Chakra Center, where the God Within dwells, awaiting you.

The following poem, from a dear friend who is now in Spirit, is a wonderful reminder of God's desire for us:

O Lord,   Let me watch to be able to see,
                Let me listen to be able to hear,
                Let me touch to be able to feel,
                Let me feel in order to know,
                Let me be humble in order to grow,
                Let me forget in order to forgive,
                Let me forgive in order to find,
                Let me pray in order to understand,
                Let me give in order to love,
O Lord,   Let me **love** in order to manifest that we are **one**.

                Baron Kili DiPauli

COMMUNICATING TRUTH - BECOMING LIGHT

The functions of talking and listening are directed by the Throat Chakra. The Fifth Chakra rules the ears, vocal chords and lung center. As we have stated earlier, the closing of the throat is what begins the vicious cycle of holding within the Heart and body miscreated thought-form energy. By opening this Center we begin to balance and harmonize ourselves. Our quality of health is uplifted towards wellness. This corresponds to our journey out of the shell of fear consciousness, the **living-to-die consciousness**, into the **living-to-heal consciousness**. The day-to-day progression of this changing attitude is evidenced in the balancing of our personal psycho-physical being.

Honest communication may take some practice. We are battling fears that have been put into Pandora's Box for years and years, and perhaps all of this misused thought-form energy may look like a dark, dirty, unlovable angry mess. This is the main reason most people do not want to ever begin to deal with these thoughtful. We are afraid of losing Love, of being unlovable, of not being accepted. Understand that this is not you; these thoughts are merely a misperception of yourself that you have chosen to keep secret for a long, long time. God sees you as perfect. There is perfection within your perceived imperfection.

We have trained ourselves not to communicate, to be separate from our brothers and sisters and from God. This hurts, and it is the hurt and loneliness that must be recognized and healed. God never hurts, God only Loves. It is our illusion that creates our "apparent" separation: the duality struggle that began when each person left the Godhead. Our inner struggle to find our identity in the right balance of the Male (yang) and the Female (yin) parts of ourselves is the fight to find our individuality. The conflict is like two halves of a sphere connected by a rubber band but seeking their own freewill. Yet, the greater desire to go in separate directions creates a greater force to bring them towards one another to reunion. When the individual surrenders and "Lets go and lets God" the battle for individuality ends. An individual is "indivisible," just as God's energy is the perfect trinity of union.

Learning to be in tune with ourselves is a joyous step-by-step process that yields abundance on all levels of existence. The hurt we may feel is contained thought-forms deep inside of Pandora's Box "kicking" their way to the surface. Be clear in knowing that these feelings are not the real you; and, therefore, do not attach yourself to them. Just let them come up and then forgive yourself. They are just bundles of nonproductive, misdirected energy seeking an avenue of expression-- and that is why they create illness. Trust in yourself and you will walk the path of illumination, where change is the only constant.

God's energy is a creative force, and no energy can be contained without seeking expression. Choose to express outwardly through Love and sharing rather than illness and retention. Open the throat and let the energy out. Bless the energy, for it too comes from God, our Divine Source of existence. Do not judge yourself, for all humans on the planet are going through the same process as you. Allow them to be your brother, and they will, in turn, do the same for you. Convert this energy into an outward directed expression of Love, Trust, Faith and Forgiveness. Find the internal connection to your God Self and "Just for today accept the many blessings" He has to offer you.

With each success and miracle of Love, we gain strength and insight to take another step. This is like learning to walk. This is a form of mobility that takes you to any level you desire to experience joy, peace, fulfillment, Love and health.

"...Until one is committed there is hesitation, the chance to draw back, always ineffectiveness. Concerning all acts of initiative (and creation), there is one elementary truth, the ignorance of which kills countless ideas and splendid plans: that moment one definitely commits oneself, then Providence moves too.

"All sorts of things occur to help one that would never otherwise have occurred. A whole stream of events issues from the decision, raising in one's favor all manner of unforeseen incidents and meetings and material assistance, which no man could have dreamt would have come his way.

"I have learned a deep respect for one of Goethe's couplets:

"'Whatever you can do, or dream you can, begin it.
Boldness has genius, power and magic in it.' "

W. H. Murry

37

CLOSING THE THROAT - THE CAUSAL FACTOR

Since our center is at the heart level, we must be able to communicate our feelings. Due to feelings of unworthiness or guilt, self-imposed or accepted, we often allow feelings of restriction and limitation to block the communicative function of the throat. So we can, and most often will, restrict at the throat chakra all that is felt emotionally "within." Closing the throat and not expressing the feelings within the heart and body is the beginning of instability in mental control of the individual's balance. This is the Causal Factor of all illness: fear to speak from the heart with unconditional love.

As we continue to contain within us more emotions, more "to-do tomorrows" are placed in "Pandora's Box;" and simple dealings become complex. We find it more difficult to understand why we are unhappy and why our body begins to produce states of unwellness.

ETHERIC ENERGY PATTERNS OF THE CHAKRAS

This diagram shows the pattern of etheric energy that results when the Throat Chakra body is blocked, holding in emotions.

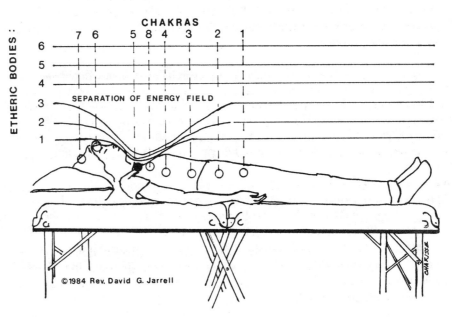

©1984 Rev. David G. Jarrell

The etheric bodies (the chakras) are layered, and they depend upon one another for their proper functions. Thoughts, emotions, external factors and foods are just some of the causes that affect each body. An imbalanced chakra body will, in turn, affect the total functioning of the person.

When we begin blocking at the throat, we limit the flow of energy from the higher etheric body-chakra centers. As time goes on, the body will become imbalanced because the hormones secreted by these upper body glands decrease. The hormones have been restricted and their output limited. So, the receptor organs and glands in the physical body below begin to dysfunction as well.

We usually find that the glands corresponding to the higher chakras are being limited in the production of hormones and that one symptom actually leads to the manifestation of other symptoms. This is the dynamics of a "Catch-22" process. When the throat blocks the connection from the higher to the lower self, an inaccurate signal sets off a complex reaction. A dysfunction in the body not only has reception of a hormone, it sends out the false message that it no longer needs that hormone. This reduces the output of the glands in question. In turn, the already imbalanced gland and subtle chakra body continues to get further out of balance. The body functions dependent upon the balanced action

38

of the glands are affected, so the spiral feeds on itself in a geometric progression that can lead to various further levels of chemical, emotional and spiritual dysfunction. We find the hormone production, chakra balance, organ function, metabolic and neurological sensitivity all moving away from a stable point of centeredness. The day-to-day requirements of living become an endless sea, filled with emotional upheavals of stress that can eventually break down a person's immunity to disease.

For example, what might happen if we are unable to express a harmoniously spiritual sharing of love with another person. We find that a blockage at the Second and the Sixth Chakras might create pains such as migraines, improper menstrual cycles, lack of menstrual cycles, the inability to attain orgasm, or pain during monthly cycles.

If someone has a migraine, we know that in addition to treating the migraine itself (a pituitary imbalance), the ovaries must be treated in a woman and the prostate in a man. By unlocking the throat, the outward flow of inner-communications, we open up the passageway for the hormones to begin their proper flow for establishing a state of harmony.

In all states of unwellness, it is imperative that we go back to the Causal Factor, the root and origin of the imbalance. The heart is the center. It is the limiting of expression and/or reception of love that is limiting the individual and causing the unwellness. To open the heart fully, to go beyond fear, is to find love. To find love is to accept the Divinity within ourselves. Only when we begin to understand that this is the passageway to harmony do we begin to take the physical body into the spiritual awakening of health.

STRESS: THE UNQUALIFIED ENERGY

Humankind came to Earth to Love and be Loved and when this does not occur, stress is the result. Stress leads to emotional disharmony, which eventually has an effect on the physical body. We must be aware of the Higher Conscious function of the Spirit in order to have balance. All lessons in life come from the past and present manifestation of unlearned lessons, and from our ability or inability to deal with them harmoniously; we either succeed or must again return to that fork in the road.

Failure to deal with lessons presented to us is the underlying factor of unwellness. Unwellness is that state of dis-ease within the physical body which affects the interrelated functions of organs and endocrine glands that provide balanced life force. We set up unwellness by not wanting to process our lesson --not wanting to release the emotions through truthful examination. We restrict the flow of Love by not wanting to take the responsibility of being the Causal Factor. No one in this world directs anything towards you that you have not asked for by unconscious or conscious thought projection.

What happens when we restrict the flow of energy? First, the Throat Chakra becomes imbalanced due to holding in the emotions of hurt, resentment, anger and ego thought - patterns that are self-destructive. These patterns radiate to everyone you meet, to the home in which you live, to the food you prepare . . . their destructive influence is unlimited.

If we close down the throat to contain the emotions, we begin to build up nonspecific energy within the physical body: if contained long enough, this becomes a physical disease. Why? Because of simply not opening up the Heart, not communicating truthfully (there is an absolute difference between speaking and communicating), not wanting to hear the inner-self screaming out for help, not dealing with it the moment the lesson began. The Heart cleanses the Mind, Body and Emotions.

Being in the flow means dealing with emotions right now, not tomorrow. If you do not take care of today, tomorrow will be just a little heavier. You will be carrying the emotional pain of yesterday and today at the same moment. So let it go, do not carry yesterday's emotions. Deal with it in the moment; bless the opportunity to gain awareness no matter what the source. Gain insight in dealing with the present and let it go. Transmute that unused unqualified energy into well directed harmoniously productive energy for happiness, joy, and Love. This is your personal responsibility. No one else has created your disharmony. Energy is in constant flow from God, and it is made positive or negative, Love or fear by you.

Life's lessons can be a growing experience in the art of loving, living in an ever expanding reality of God's intended happiness, joy, and wellness. We only need to continue learning each and every day to live in spiritual aspiration, knowing that each day brings more opportunities to test how we transform and use the energy of God's Unconditional Love.

Spirituality is the ever-expanding spiral of the vortex of transformed light radiating from each of our Chakra Centers, ever-expanding, never-ending, infinite as the cosmos of creation. It is a path of thought-forms guiding us closer and closer to the harmony of the celestial sounds of peace and harmony, guiding us along the etheric field of energy lines in our sleep and meditations, to be returned to the conscious mind - body - spirit as etheric fuel for the soul's journey, knowing the day will come when the personality will no longer be a burden, but will be a vehicle to experience the Divine Light of a matter: Divine Form.

In the spiritual consciousness all matter transcends the perceived reality of the unconscious man. As we learn to personify and live the example of the Living God Consciousness others who come into contact with our aura will be transformed. This is the path of Spirituality. It is not a place, nor a thing we can grasp. It is the essence of the unseen, yet felt, energy of God motivating us further and further beyond our imagination. It is the spark of life; it is Light and Love.

Chapter Five

ATTUNEMENT: THE **Reiki Plus**® TREATMENT

Treating Self

Through the use of Reiki for self-healing, the individual receives a Spiritual uplifting, upgrades his body stamina, and influences his entire consciousness.

A daily Reiki treatment brings about an inner attunement with the emotions, so that they can more easily be dealt with. Harmful emotions come from threats to our ego, our fear center. The focus of **Reiki Plus**® is Loving the Self and the God within us. When we Love our total Self and accept our co-creative God-Presence, our ego-fear is no longer in control: "Thy will be done" is then personal consciousness expanding in Divine Will.

Reiki provides you the focus to productively direct your feelings, desires and human needs, to transcend your human state of limitation, into the unlimited state of Love, happiness and joy. God, the ultimate source of Reiki, has always desired His Divine Plan of Happiness, Joy and Love to be made manifest in the hearts of all humankind; however, humankind has not always been willing to take full responsibility for individual actions. This irresponsible attitude creates separation, fear and limitation in the use of God's unlimited, free-flowing energy: The Holy Breath.

The use of Reiki in our personal lives offers a means of balance, so that we can attain a healthy Mind, Body and Emotions. If we choose this path to open ourselves to our Divine Self, we will find that all true Spiritual philosophy is without contradiction. Reiki gives us the means of tapping an infinite source of healing energy and to use it to be totally responsible for our lives, to be totally Divine in all of life's pleasures and challenges.

Treating Another Person

Reiki energy comes from the God-source through the focus of those Masters of Reiki who are in Spirit form. When we, as **Reiki Plus**® Practitioners, place our hands on another person (as when we place them on ourselves), we become attuned to the healing Ray of Reiki .

The Reiki energy enters our higher heart center, the Eighth Chakra, the Sixth Etheric Body. This healing energy opens our physical heart center (4th Chakra) to receive the healing energy through the Crown (7th Chakra).

As the energy flows into our Heart centers, our bodies begins to fill up with healing energy. This is stored as a reserve in the physical body. The Healer is also receiving a healing energy while giving a healing to the Healee. A **Reiki Plus**® Practitioner, has greater energy after the healing than before.

In Reiki healing there is only the giving (a flowing through) of energy through the healer to the healee. **We do not take pain away by taking it into our own energy field or into our own body.** To take on or pull into you the healee's pain or emotions is in direct contradiction of Reiki. (This is further discussed in the next section on attunement.) Reiki provides energy balancing for the harmonizing of the body, mind and emotions of all who receive this healing Light.

ATTUNEMENT TO THE HEALEE'S PAIN

It is not uncommon to become attuned to the healee's pain. Normally, its registration in the healer is in the same body part or area as the pain in the healee. However, this does not mean the healer is taking on, or will keep the pain.

The registration level is, in fact, a barometer effect; telling you, the Healer, how much energy the client will require to balance the energy in the imbalanced or pained area. As the pain subsides and balance returns, the pain level in your own body part will also diminish until both of you are free of any indications of pain or energy imbalances.

Reiki Plus® is **not** a system of extraction nor the taking on of pain from the healee. If you find that you are being left with pain once the healing is completed, then you have personally desired (consciously or unconsciously) to retain the other person's psycho-physical imbalance. I have found this to be a common habit of people born under the dominant astrological influences of Pisces and Cancer. If your Natal (birth) planets Sun, Moon, ascendant or Venus are in either of those two zodiacal signs or these natal planets reside in the house of Pisces (the 12th house) or Cancer (the 4th house), then you are born sensitive. This sensitivity, when developed, leads to the perception level called clairsentience, clear feeling. Clarity occurs when one can distinctly distinguish the origin of the energy and control the influence it projects.

Learning to know the difference between one's own feelings, pains and energy balance from and radiated by another person or a collective energy source takes training. A very simple procedure is to ask an objective question to place oneself in an objective frame of mind; i.e., "What is the source of this energy I am experiencing." This is important, since feelings (energy) affect us on subjective levels before manifesting in an objective or distinguishable form, such as a pain in a specific area. It is, however, important to remember that projected energy may register within you, changing your own happy mood to one less vibrant or even sad. This type of reception registers then on a more subjective level. In this situation it's (more) difficult to pinpoint that the personal energy shift has been caused by your response to an external projection of energy, whether this projection was directed specifically to you or not.

The objective question then is to ask yourself, "Is this my own emotion, or am I being sensitized by an outside source of energy?" Take a moment to step outside of yourself when you ask this question. Clarity can be attained in this manner. Of course, practice is the greatest teacher.

An important point to remember in healing is that we strongly suggest a meditative prayer before you begin the healing. This sets up the proper energy shield around you to protect you from becoming emotionally involved on a sympathetic level; but it does not prevent you from registering the imbalanced areas of the healee.

Your ability to sense in your own body the imbalances within the healee is a developed state of conscious awareness. It is an excellent tool to guide you in providing total balance to each part of the healee's body.

Remember, the registration in our own body subsides, along with the sensation in our hands, when the proper amount of **Reiki Plus**® energy has been given to the healee.

KNOW YOU ARE LIGHT

A protective technique is to surround yourself with "White Light" before a healing or entering into a new or strange environment. With practice this technique it will soon become an automatic (subconscious) action. When we realize that we are Light and really have no need to place Light around us, we have attained a higher level of awareness.

We are more subject to reacting to another's energy when we are tired, trustingly open, or naive to false exteriors of another person's ulterior motives. If this occurs, simply stop for a few moments and project the Light from within you, and make it expand to a greater distance around you.

To project this Light, start first by remembering that darkness cannot overshadow Light. So, from within your Heart Center radiate White Light in a vertical, clockwise pattern (if left-handed, counterclockwise) around your heart. As it intensifies and expands the physical chest cavity with a greater volume of energy, allow it to go into the Solar Plexus (the fear center of ego insecurity) and the adrenal glands. Bring the energy up through the throat to the top of the head while it descends through the lower centers, legs and feet. When this is accomplished, radiate the Light around you like a white cocoon.

During this visualization process, silently project from your Mind to your body and surroundings that you are

Love and a spark of God, that nothing can harm you, nor can it enter permanently into your Soul-Spirit-Body energy field.

This technique can be used at any time and for any need you may have. However, the more attuned we become to the God-Presence, the more we know and remember that we are Light. The Light never leaves us; however, we may foolishly choose to forget God's Presence and not allow the Light to be a conscious part of our existence.

You are the Light - the intensity of your Light depends upon your acceptance and focus of God's Presence.

THE HEALING SETTING

The setting:

The room in which you do healing should be conducive to harmonious energy patterns. This includes the decoration: colors may be soft blues, purples, and greens, with pink highlights. This is not mandatory for the healing to be effective. It is, however, relaxing to the healee and helps you to attune to a healing state of mind. Reiki will work on a busy street, an airplane, or anywhere else.

The comfort of the healee and the healer:

It is best to have a healing table the proper height for you to either sit or stand during the healing. The proper table provides comfort for both people. This is especially important since the treatment might last an hour or more. If a healing table is not available, a dining room table with a foam pad or folded blankets will work just fine. If the healee is bedridden, then position him so you can reach him without discomfort. Keeping your back straight is less tiring and allows a better flow of energy than bending over for a long period of time. If you are not comfortable, you will most likely not be as attuned to the healee as you would like to be.

Use your imagination to design a suitable healing platform when your normal facilities are not available. The floor is the least desirable for the comfort of the healer; but if it is the only available place, then use it.

Clothing:

The healee is to remain clothed during the healing session. It is suggested that jewelry, belts with large metal buckles, shoes, or binding outer garments be removed.

During the healing session be sure that you provide the client with adequate cover for warmth when resting. Remember, Reiki radiates heat, and when the hands change location a cooling takes place. If the room is cool, it can be chilling to the client, so cover him with a light-weight covering. (This can be the case even in the summer months.)

Hygiene:

Always wash your hands and arms before a healing and after a healing. In the case of treating an open infection, wear protective sterile rubber gloves. If these are not available, then either keep the hands off the afflicted body area, or place a sterile gauze bandage over the area if you must make contact with the body. If you, the healer have an open cut or infected area on your hand, then wear sterile gloves or do not give a treatment until it is totally healed.

Keep the entire treatment area in a high state of cleanliness.

Music:

Meditative music is most conducive to relaxing both the healee and the healer. Harp and flute are by far the best instruments, capable of harmonizing one's subtle emotional energies. This will open the healee to a higher state of receptivity and enhance the rate of healing. Some electronic music is agreeable to the subtle energy of healing; discre-

43

tion must be used in selecting music, since much electronic music is not harmonic with the subtle bodies, the chakras.

Use of Gem Stones:

I have found that an amethyst, placed under the healing table, is an excellent means of radiating transmuting energy. There are many gem stones that can be used for specific types of physical, mental, and emotional disorders. I suggest you research these in books on this subject if you need additional information.

The Healer's attunement before the healing:

It is most important that you be in a state of inward harmony. Be "centered." When you are fully attuned to the purpose of being an open channel for healing, then a greater quantity of energy can flow through you to the healee. Reiki always works, unless you are blocked; however, if the healer is in a harmonious state, then the healee will relax much faster. Our auras instantly express our state of Mind, Body, and Emotions.

If you intend to practice healing on a regular basis, it is good to have a special area of the house where all that you do is heal and meditate. The energy will remain in the room and begin to charge it with greater healing energy each time you work in it. Keep it free of unpleasant vibrations.

Cleansing the Room: before and after a healing session

Burning Sage is an excellent purifier for removing old or undesirable energy.
Sage does leave a pleasant aroma in the room.

Epson Salt and alcohol (rubbing) mixed in a damp mixture can be burned in a non flammable container. It transmutes any negative or remaining emotion residue from the healee. It works on the chemical principle of magnesium being released from the magnesium sulfate (Epson salt) by the energy of fire. It is parallel to the functional properties of an amethyst stone, which is purple due to the presence of magnesium. Magnesium is the mineral of the Heart Chakra.

Invocation of Healing:

I like to burn a white candle as a representation of God's Presence when I do a healing. A black candle is never to be used in healing. The white candle represents the "Flame of God's Light."

A Prayer to Invite the Christ Presence into the Healing

Pray at the beginning of the healing. I find it very conducive to say a prayer just after placing my hands on the healee. Prayer is a very special tool for attuning the Healer and Healee to the purpose and intent of the healing session.

Often, this prayer comes to Heart:

Mother-Father God, whose Light dwells in the hearts of all creation, may this Light and the Christ Presence surround us, protect us and flow through us. That this Thy child (...insert healee's name...) have a complete and irreversible healing, of (his/her) mind, body and emotions. That (...name of healee...) open his/her heart to experience and participate in the responsibility of this healing, knowing that all healings are as successful as the healee utilizes the incoming Christ Presence from You. In Thy name we pray.

The treatment:

Treat the entire body. You have been directed to precounsel the client to understand the imbalance; and, that three or more sessions are required to complete the initial energy balancing of the "healing curve." However, treat as many times (sessions) as are required to heal the person.

Treat the affected area(s) as long as the Reiki energy continues to be drawn through your hands before moving to another area. Your hands will always indicate when balance of an organ, endocrine gland, bone or muscle has been reached. Do not move until this release is allowed by the diminishing of the energy, sensation, or magnetic pull from the area being treated.

Reiki will work even if you are not able to touch the body due to the nature of the injury or emotional status of the healee. This is true especially in the case of third degree burns, open wounds, or other injuries not advisable to touch due to the healee's potential discomfort, or danger of infection.

Touching: A professional attitude:

Do not touch the private, reproductive areas of the healee. It is not necessary to make direct contact with the healee's body for Reiki to enter into it.

In the event that the healee directs his or her Second Chakra energy to create or allow physical arousal, simply think the color pink. Project the pink color over the healee to balance the Second Chakra and redirect it's energy to a universal love response. If the healee is not responsive to this "pink technique," bend his knees by raising them off the table while resting his feet on the table.

We have to realize not everyone you heal is totally balanced in his consciousness. Many people mistake Universal Love for physical desire. Reiki is a touching, gentle Love. It gives you an opportunity to help your clients expand their awareness, to understand that touching has many levels in expressing Love.

Talking during the healing:

Quiet conversation can be helpful, especially if the healee feels like opening up and discussing the emotions surrounding the state of his or her unwellness. Do not feel it necessary to investigate the cause if your client does not feel in touch with or inclined to talk about such feelings.

There are times when emotional discussions can be inhibiting to the healing process, causing unnecessary tension, pain, and remorse. Since Reiki works on all levels of the Body, Mind, and Emotions, do not feel that you, as the healer are required to counsel. When you provide the Reiki healing energy to take away his physical pain, the client will in his own time, go inward, and begin to consciously touch with the emotional factors that have resulted in this particular unwellness.

Distracting noise, children playing, and TV are not conducive to the healing session. If you must be interrupted to have a conversation, it is best to go outside the healing room. Use your discretion.

Hand Pressure:

Relax your hands and gently place on the body in the appropriate position. Any pressure or heaviness from your hands will be a discomfort to the healee.

To insure your hands are relaxed, you must be comfortable. If you are straining from where you are sitting or standing, then reposition. As I have so often said, "If you are not comfortable, it ain't Reiki." Unless you are unstrained, you will be thinking more of your discomfort than the Reiki flowing into the healee. You will then find yourself shifting from a healing consciousness to an attitude of 'when can I finish'. The healing setting must include your own comfort, except in an emergency when the healee's needs must completely outweigh any of your own.

It is important to consider the needs of the client. There are many variables due to the differences of the individuals you will treat. I will list those which are consistent with most clients.

1. Is the room temperature too warm or too cold? The temperature should be comfortable. A cold draft from air conditioning or an open window might chill the healee. As he will be warmed by the healing energy, an uncovered

area just treated is subject to cooling rapidly; therefore, if it is winter or the room is cool, place a light blanket on the person.

2. Does he need a pillow under his head? Some people desire a pillow for comfort.

3. Does he need a pillow under the knees? A pillow under the knees takes pressure off of the lower spinal area. People suffering from lower back problems or women with a tipped uterus will need pillows under their knees. A pregnant woman will need to be treated lying on her side. Place a pillow (or pillows) under the fetus for comfort, and place a pillow between her legs. She will be your best guide, so ask her what she needs.

Above all, help your client be comfortable in the healing setting. The temperature, the lighting, the music and many other factors will need consideration. Experience will give you additional ideas of how to best provide for the needs of your clients. Be loving: this is the most important factor. The client is with you to be loved. Reiki is love. It flows into your Christ Center from God. Be then in the state of Grace and enjoy the experience of sharing God's Unconditional Divine Love. Clear your mind and "Let go and Let God."

THE HEALING CURVE

The healing curve is the time period that an illness requires to reverse itself to a state of health (wellness). A physical unwellness is unbalanced energy within the emotional, mental, higher conscious, and spiritual etheric bodies that has manifested in the physical body. The location of the unwellness is directly related to the imbalance "above" which has resided in the body "below."

All states of physical anatomical unwellness correspond to an esoteric anatomical emotional misalignment that has not been dealt with properly. In other words, the "tic marks" in Pandora's Box have begun to overflow into the body, and to affect its functioning. Unresolved stress produces a sickness (pathology), a result of the trauma.

We work with these "awakened" traumas by realizing the person's physical energy. However, the emotional stage is dealt with, on more subtle levels in most cases. In the following material I will present the various levels of cleansing that take place simultaneously within the healee. Remember that we work on three levels; Body, Mind, and Emotions, and that the energy of Reiki, through the modality of **Reiki Plus®**, effects multidimensional changes. These changes need to be understood so that the practitioner is able to help the healee work through the realignment period with a positive frame of mind.

Elimination of Pain Through Proper Treatments

Physical disorders fall into one of three general categories (degrees of imbalance): **Acute** (inflammatory); **Sub-acute** (less inflammatory); **Chronic** (a lingering condition). When we begin Reiki treatments, the client will go through these three conditions as stages of the healing process. No matter what category he may be in at the beginning of the healing process, he will experience first acute, then sub-acute, and then chronic symptoms. The average period of time is three days if treatments are given three days in a row. The reason for the three treatments in a row for problematic physical imbalances (pathological disorders) is to quickly establish the balance, while eliminating any pains, aches and toxins from the body.

So, the commitment of both the healee and the healer must include scheduling three treatments in a row; also, that subsequent treatments will be given at regular intervals thereafter. A person reaches a state of health by progressively reestablishing energy patterns in the direction of a balance which results in a continued production of healthy energy.

To treat haphazardly or inconsistently, in most cases, is to stir up energy blockages with ineffectual results. This is worse than not treating the person at all. In fact, if the client is unwilling to make a commitment, do not begin treatment without explaining the procedure and making it clear that results depend upon the healee's participation and commitment to becoming healthy. Refer to the "Contract to Healing Bulletin."

Starting up the Motor

When the body parts begin to be stimulated by the healing energy one of the more common responses is, "It hurts more." Actually, this might not be the whole truth. The body is a fine-tuned instrument which works in a way that is both simple and complex; each part has a specific function; yet many parts jointly support one another in an emergency. We can also look at the body as a car engine to help us see the analogy of "starting up" an imbalanced or dysfunctional part or organ.

A new piston in an old engine must become tuned and broken-in before it will run smoothly. The same is true for an imbalanced part of the body, yet it reacts a little differently. As the balancing begins, the nerves send messages to the brain saying, "I feel different down here." What they are actually saying is, "I am beginning to function." The awareness of pain is the "awakening" of the nerves, tissues and blood supply in the imbalanced area, beginning the release of toxins (thought-forms). At the same time replacement of nutrients, proper body chemical balancing and reorganizing the biochemistry towards a healthy status begin.

The acute stage is the beginning registration of change in the body, the start of its journey towards wellness and health. This leads us to a purification process and through the three stages of the healing curve. This is explained in the following section on toxicity-purification.

Toxicity - Purification Process

When the Reiki energy enters the body there is a large-scale release of toxic materials held in dead or malfunctioning cells in inert or non-circulating body fluids, in blocked lymphatic structures, and in the debris of tissue breakdown. The tissues and organs storing toxins (thought-forms) in the body will be points where, during healing, neurological sensitivity will be prominent. As the balancing energy enters the body, it will begin to stimulate the imbalanced parts, stirring up varying reactions.

One of the most common reactions comes from the actual toxin removal as they are released into the cardiovascular and lymphatic system and then into the lungs, liver, skin, and gastrointestinal tract for elimination. A major part of this release of accumulated toxins comes from the liver.

This release, more often than not, at first causes the healee being treated to feel worse than before the treatment began. It must be understood that the entire body will detoxify in direct proportion to the amount of toxins it holds. This is the "Inflammatory or Acute" stage of the healing. In fact, it is not uncommon for a person to have a flare-up, somewhat worse than existed before the treatment. The degree of the acuteness tells us how toxic the client really is. If it occurs throughout the body and is not localized to the imbalanced area, then we can safely assume that the level of psycho-physical imbalance has been present for some time period, or that the client has recently been on a diet highly toxic to his metabolism.

As the treatments continue into the second and third day, the body will continue to improve; as balanced energy displaces imbalanced energy.

This section would hardly be complete without a mention of a most neglected part of the body, the gastrointestinal tract. The intestines always play a major role: toxic buildup in the body. The gastrointestinal tract has a very important function in our health maintenance. Unfortunately, it is the area most often overlooked. If this has been true in your life, or the client's, then I hope the following words will impress upon you new insight and respect for the small and large intestines and the importance of frequent bowel movements.

First, let me state that I concur with Dr. Bernard Jensen, D.C. and Dr. Robert Gray that physical illness is directly related to the condition of the GI tract. Secondly, let us not forget synchronistic parallels on each level of unwellness: the whole is made up of the parts.

Many people believe, "We are what we eat." This may not always hold true, but it does suggest that any attraction to the wrong foods will continually stimulate imbalance. We see this in the allergy condition where an individual will crave the food allergen that will trigger an allergic reaction, creating stress, trauma and specific physical and emotional symptoms.

People who eat allergy stimulating foods that are mucus-forming begin to limit the function of the intestinal tract in several ways. Foods are not properly digested, nor their nutrients absorbed through the intestinal wall lining due to the excess mucus. When mucus foods are consumed in larger quantities than raw vegetables, fruits, juices, water, and other non-mucus-forming foods, the mucus accumulation on the colon walls begins. If our diet is balanced with 60% raw foods and our colon is clean from at least semiannual fasting, then two bowel movements daily will be normal. Painful, hard, or infrequent bowel movements that do not break apart when the toilet is flushed, contain too much mucus. Continued diets of this nature contribute to placing the body in a sensitive state. At this stage, a psycho-physical imbalance sets the stage for the illness it desires and needs.

Since it's difficult in Western culture to eat without the consumption of mucus forming foods, it is considered a good health practice to eat enough raw vegetables, and to drink plenty of water and natural juices (juices should be diluted 50% with water to reduce the sugar content).

It is generally considered that herbal capsules and teas of Comfrey-Pepsin or Comfrey-Fenugreek are beneficial for breaking up mucus in the system. Cayenne Pepper, uncooked, is also an excellent demucusing agent for the lungs and bowels.

"The total volume of fluid that enters the small intestines each day is about 9 liters...This fluid is derived from ingestion of fluids (about 1.5 liters) and from various gastrointestinal secretions (about 7.5 liters). Roughly 8 to 8.5 liters of the fluid in the small intestines is absorbed; the remainder, about 0.5 to 1.0 liters passes into the large intestines. There most of it is absorbed. The absorption of water by the small intestines occurs by osmosis... through epithelial cells... The normal rate of absorption is about 200 to 400 ml./hr. Water can move across the intestinal mucosa in both directions. The absorption of water from the small intestines is associated with the absorption of electrolytes and digested foods in order to maintain an osmotic balance with the blood."

Tortora and Anagnostakos
Principles of Anatomy and Physiology, 4th Ed. p. 617

Baths for Detoxification and Pain

Cleansing the body of toxins, tension and pain can be facilitated by the use of a bath. If you or your client are experiencing muscle pain or swollen tissue, use 1 cup of Epson salts in a tub of hot water for a 20 minute soak.

If the client is toxic with emotional stress, then have him use 1 pound of table salt and 1 pound of bicarbonate of soda in hot bath water. If the client has fear or symptoms similar thereto, then suggest he only stays in the bath for a "comfortable" period of time, 20 minutes will be the objective. The frequency of detoxifying baths can be regulated according to the need of the client. Have the client take a bath after the initial healing and there after, when they feel the need. The mental, physical and emotional equilibrium will benefit.

Clients have shared that the salt-soda bath does clear the residual feelings and thoughts acknowledged and/or confronted during the healing session. If your client is on fragile footing, suggest the bath to last within his emotional comfort zone. A 20 minute rest in total quiet afterwards is part of the treatment.

"Thought-Forms" - the illusions of the emotions made physical

The trauma is not only emotional stress. The intellect has put forth enough "Thought-Forms" for them to now reside as a foreign element in the body; i.e., infection, cancer, calcium deposits, dysfunctional body parts, etc. We create in physical reality (our illusion) an imbalanced condition that "mirrors" the etheric body imbalances. Of course, we cannot forget that our Heart is our center and through it we always respond (consciously or unconsciously). Therefore, our "Thought-Forms" have a direct correspondence to how we feel about ourselves, to love and, its opposite, fear.

When a person brings down from the etheric levels imbalances of emotional energy (fear vs. love) in the form of Thought-Forms, the body begins to set up, unconsciously, complex reactions that stimulate this imbalance. This stimulation is on all levels of our existence: food to create nutritional deficiencies; relations (friends or lovers) to stimulate the heart and set up mirrored responses disliked, yet consciously unrecognized, by the person; environmental influences that add fuel to fire the condition; and, thought patterns that provide confronting situations to force recognition of the true Causal Factor of the imbalance (unwellness, pathology, etc.): the person himself.

The bottom line, then, in all pathologies, be they physical, emotional, or mental, is first and foremost the person's inability to Love himself by maintaining his consideration of personal unworthiness, guilt, and having been born in "Original Sin." The most difficult to apply and, therefore, the most important **Reiki Plus** ® Principle is, "Just For Today I Will Accept My Many Blessings." This means to accept the Self. To Love the Self. To allow the "I AM" Christ Consciousness to become illumined and the "Christ-Self" to begin radiating inside the heart, embrace the physical body and glorify the "God-Self."

It is by this simple process, to see ourselves worthy of God's Love and Blessings, that unwellness is transformed into happiness, joy, peace, Love and wellness. Take a moment and think about this -- we are all Light, the Light of God, and God made us in His Perfect Image. The God of Light is not a God of wrath, fire, and damnation. God is Love, Peace and Joy. Mankind has created a fear of God by man's judgment values that are used to control the judicious and prudent Divine free will actions of mankind. We must remember: God has only two Laws and man has thousands. God's Laws simply say, "Love the Lord thy God with all thy Heart and with all thy Soul and with all thy Mind; and Love thy neighbor as thy self." So simple that few humans have truly mastered the understanding in Body, Mind and Emotions (Heart, Mind and Soul connected by Spirit).

It is through the higher vibrations of Love, the God-Presence level of the Heart (8th Chakra), that Divine Will can manifest and humankind become free of toxic thoughts of guilt and fear. It is, therefore, essential that Love becomes the guiding Light in all aspects of one's life for health, happiness and joy to be a reality of human existence.

Chapter Six

FASTING

The benefits and purposes of fasting are many in the maintenance of health, prevention of physical disorders, and cleansing during unwellness. There are also as many opinions about "how to fast" as there are types of fasts and why, when, and how long one should fast. It is suggested that you research the subject if you wish to learn about the wide spectrum of opinions.

This Chapter presents to you a fasting procedure which can be utilized for removing mucus from the GI tract and also for removing gallbladder stone removal.

Please take note that if you have any questions as to whether you should or should not fast, please contact a qualified, licensed holistic practitioner: medical doctor, chiropractor, or nutritionist. There are cases, such as diabetes, where a person should only fast under the supervision of a qualified specialist; or not fast if so advised.

The following fasting format is a generally accepted process that will, under normal circumstances, result in a greater yield of energy, higher standard of nutrition and food absorption in the intestines.

Fasting - Preparation

The body must be prepared for a fast. To begin fasting without proper preparation will disrupt the body's natural rhythm. This is not the purpose of fasting. The purpose is to cleanse the body of mucus, toxins, and gallbladder stones while improving the overall level of health and wellbeing.

How to prepare the Body and Mind depends on your present diet. If you are a heavy consumer of meat, cheese, wheat, dairy products (milk, yogurt, cream, butter-cow or goat), sugars, caffeine, candy, eggs, and chocolate, your preparation time will be greater than that of a person who consumes few or none of these foods. Preparation consists of eliminating these mucus-forming foods from the diet at a moderate rate. While gradually eliminating these foods, you want to establish the proper frequency of bowel movements, two or three per day. Eating Reiki slaw twice a day (described below) and drinking 6-8 glasses of water will begin to establish this frequency. Non-mucus producing foods are consumed during this elimination period.

Once all mucus foods are eliminated from the diet, you will be able to tell when you are ready for the next step. To know this you must inspect your bowel movements. What you are looking for is to know when you are passing mucus-free stools. A mucoid-free stool is fully formed and will break up when the toilet is flushed. This does not mean loose stools.

It is important to note is when you finish passing old, dried stools that come from accumulated mucus on the lining of the GI tract. These stools are putrid in odor and often times have the appearance of compressed squares of old fecal matter. This is what prevents proper absorption of nutrients from foods and supplements.

So you have cleaned the mucoid stools from the colon with the slaw, water, and elimination of mucous foods. Your diet now consists of raw vegetables, sprouts, juices, fruit, and some grains and nuts. Now, you can begin the actual fast to cleanse the toxins from the blood, liver, lymph and cells of the body and then to flush out any gallstones you may have.

The Fasting Foods

Raw, unpasteurized apple juice from apples grown organically is your best choice. Your purpose is to remove toxins, not put in additional ones while fasting. The apple juice should be diluted with spring or chemical-free water in equal parts. Unless directed by a Practitioner, I do not feel that distilled water is good for everyone; whether you are fasting or not. Distilled water requires that you replace the trace mineral salts missing from it. This can be accomplished with Sea Water or homeopathic multiple tissue salts.

You need to drink (slowly) not less than eight 12 oz. glasses of juice per day and eat at least 1 cup of the Reiki slaw per day, more if you desire. Water can also be consumed as desired.

REIKI SLAW

Ingredients: Green cabbage, cauliflower, raw beets, celery, garlic and onion. Grate equal amounts of cabbage and cauliflower. This will keep in a sealed container for a week or so. Then, when you are ready to eat, grate raw beet(s), chop celery (garlic and onion to your taste, or you may omit). I also add raw sunflower seeds.

Dressing: sesame seed oil (sunflower or cold-pressed olive oils are fine), apple cider vinegar, water, and herbs to taste.

Eat 1/2 cup twice daily for cleansing intestines of mucous. The slaw can be eaten as you would a salad, each day with a meal, or as your only food for cleansing when fasting.

The purpose of the slaw is to maintain your bowel movements every day of the fast. When you fast, you must have at least one bowel movement each day. If you elect to not eat the slaw, you will need to have an enema each evening to remove the toxins from the colon. Do not forget that fasting means to cleanse the body of toxins, and many of them go directly into the colon. Unless removed, the toxins from the liver, blood and lymph glands will cause a greater imbalance and physical reaction in the Mind and Body than existed before you began the fast. They have, so to speak, been stored away and not affecting the body, as they will radically when released by fasting.

The Fasting Steps

The day before you start the fast, eat only raw fruit to help cleanse away any foods in the system. Drink plenty of water and apple juice. Fast for three days on the juice and slaw. When you finish the fast, do not eat a heavy meal. If your first meal is brown rice and steamed vegetables your body will respond more favorably than if you eat heavily. Do not begin eating excessive amounts of mucus foods. In fact, you may actually find that your body does not desire them as much as before, or possibly not at all.

You can help maintain the elimination of mucus by using the herb Comfrey, as tea or in capsules, combined with Pepsin or Fenugreek. These (Comfrey and Pepsin) are digestive aids and stimulate proper bowel movements.

Gallstones

There are two types of stones. "Traditionally gallstones have been classified according to their composition. This information was then used to demonstrate the cause of the stone formation. This is no longer considered valid. Generally the core of all gallstones contains a mixture of cholesterol, bilirubin and protein (Tabers Encyclopedia Medical Dictionary, 12th Ed. 1973, p. G-3.)." One comes from high carbohydrate consumption and they are called the "green stringies." Most people have some of them unless they are on a carbohydrate-free diet, which is rather rare under normal circumstances. The second type is calcium-formed stones and these come from a high acid metabolism and diet. Each type of stone requires a different fasting juice for being broken down in the gallbladder. The first type, carbohydrate stones, use the Apple Juice Fast previously described. Non-meat eaters tend to have an alkaline metabolism and consume larger amounts of carbohydrates for energy.

For the second type, calcium stones, use the Lemon Juice and Water Fast. If you are a heavy meat eater, drink a lot of sodas, have an acid metabolism, or have been diagnosed by your physician as having calcium stones, then use the

Lemon Juice and Water for three days. Do not, I repeat, do not add maple syrup to the lemon water. It shifts the sugar-insulin balance and will cause hypoglycemia in persons who are not hypoglycemic. You will follow the same fasting procedure as previously given for three days for both types of stones.

Flushing the Stones

In the early morning of the third day take 4 oz's of Cold-Pressed Olive Oil. Wash it down with a hot cup of water into which one or more lemons have been squeezed. Go back to bed, lie in the fetal position on your right side and rest. You will normally have a bowel movement within 3-4 hours. Plan to spend the day resting or at home until you have finished moving your bowels. Continue to drink the fasting juice during the day.

When you begin to eat, follow the suggestions in the preceding section.

How Often To Fast

It is considered a good practice to fast at least twice a year; at the end of winter and of summer, as we shift diets according to growing seasons and changes of climate. Fasting more often than this should be done with moderation. Many people fast monthly, others every change of season. However, if you feel your body becoming toxic or mucoid, it is a good idea to fast whenever this happens.

Fasting one day a week actually requires three days: a day each of preparation, of fasting, and readjusting. In many cases it is not wise for a person to fast in this manner, as it does tend to deplete the body of energy. If you feel inclined to extreme fasting, please consult a qualified health or medical practitioner. You may do more harm than good. Also, do not fast with just water unless directed by a qualified practitioner.

If you have any questions about your metabolism type, requirements and fasting needs, consult a qualified nutritionist, physician, chiropractor, or health care practitioner.

Chapter Seven

THE TREATMENT: HAND POSITION DIAGRAMS

Self-Treatment Positions for the Head

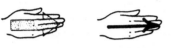

The arrow point is the direction your fingers are to point.

Place hands against your body without pressure.

RH: Right Hand
LH: Left Hand

POSITION #1:

Hands cover the front of the face, with the tips of the fingers touching the hair line or the top of the forehead. Hands are abutted. Be sure to cover the nose.

POSITION #2:

The tips of the middle fingers are placed on the crown of the head. Allow the fingers and hands to gently rest on the head.

POSITION #3:

The heels of the hands are cupped under the occiput bones at the lower portion of the skull (where the skull ends and the neck begins). The fingers extend straight upwards with the thumbs and index fingers touching. If this is awkward, use the alternate position described below:

POSITION #3 ALTERNATE:

Place hands horizontally behind the head. One hand is above the occiput ridge, and the other below.

POSITION #4:

The LH is placed at the neck and rests on the chest, with the RH on the chest directly below.

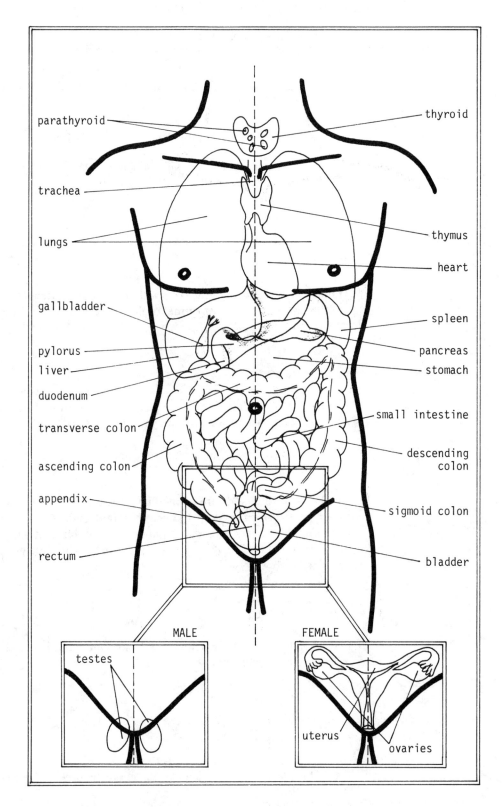

parathyroid

thyroid

trachea

lungs

thymus

heart

gallbladder

spleen

pylorus

pancreas

liver

stomach

duodenum

transverse colon

small intestine

ascending colon

descending colon

appendix

sigmoid colon

rectum

bladder

MALE

FEMALE

testes

uterus

ovaries

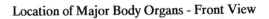

Location of Major Body Organs - Front View

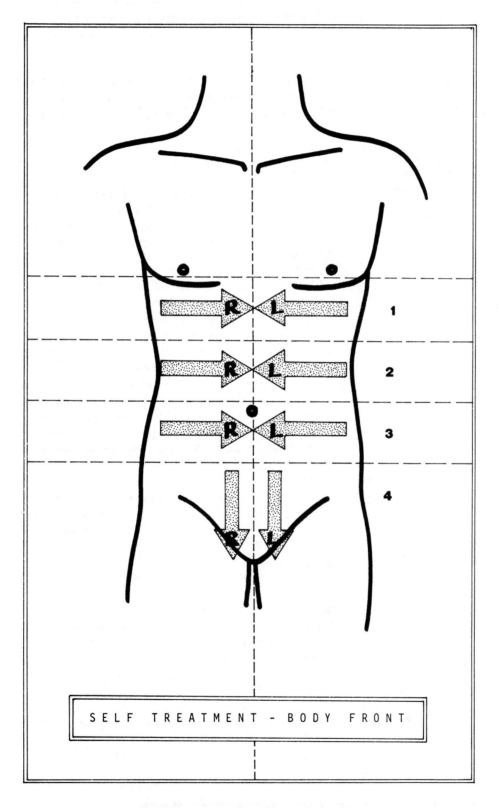

SELF TREATMENT - BODY FRONT

Self-Treatment Hand Positions: Body - Front

POSITION FOR TREATING BREAST

Place hands to cover the entire breast.

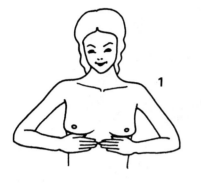

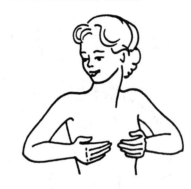

POSITION #1:

Hands are placed under the breast line with middle fingertips touching. Hands are placed gently on the body. Fingertips abut the center-line of the body.

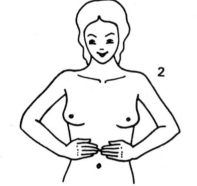

POSITION #2:

One hand-width down. The lower edge of the hands should be resting on the waistline.

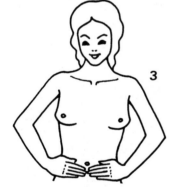

POSITION #3:

Thumbs along the waistline, one hand width down from #2.

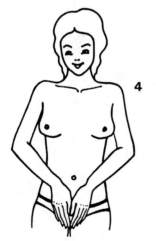

POSITION #4:

Hands pointed down. Thumbs and index fingers are touching. Fingertips touch the pubic bone.

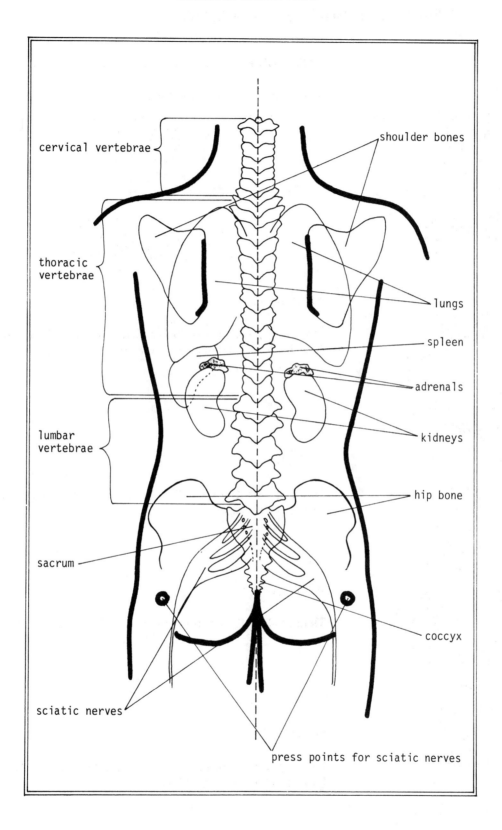

cervical vertebrae

shoulder bones

thoracic
vertebrae

lungs

spleen

adrenals

kidneys

lumbar
vertebrae

hip bone

sacrum

coccyx

sciatic nerves

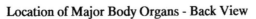

press points for sciatic nerves

Location of Major Body Organs - Back View

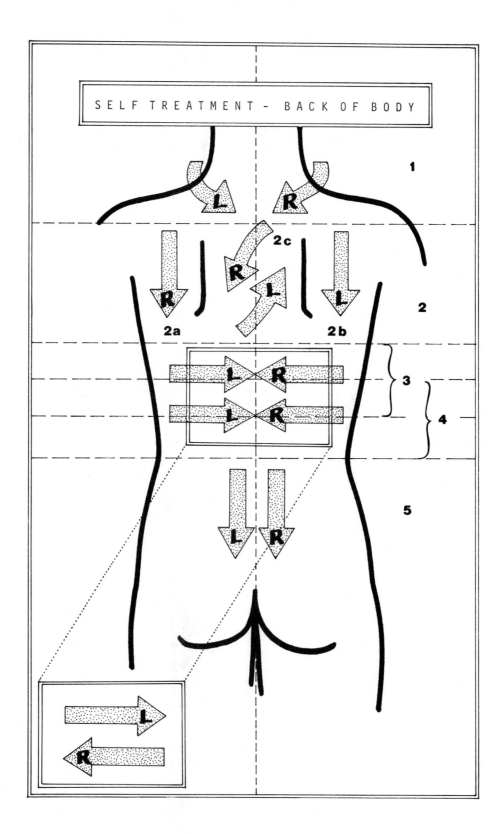

Self-Treatment Hand Positions; Body - Back

Self-Treatment Positions for the Back

POSITION #1:

Reach up and place hands on the shoulder muscles, while the middle fingertips touch the channel of the spine. (The indentation on either side of the centerline of the spine.)

POSITION #2:

There are three separate moves in this position:

a. With RH reach across, in front of body, and place the RH on the left shoulder blade; then after balancing the shoulder blade, lower your arm and...

b. with the LH reach across, in front of body, and place LH on the right shoulder blade; then, after balancing the right shoulder blade...

c. reach around and behind the back with the LH; and then place RH on the opposite side of the spine. Place both hands between the shoulder blades with fingers touching.

POSITIONS 3 and 4 combined:

With knuckles of the hand over the centerline guide as a, place one above the other; the hands are equally covering each side of the spine. The lower hand rests at the waistline.

POSITION #5:

Hands pointed downward, edges of hands and little fingers touching; heels of the hand at the waistline and middle fingertips touching the tip of the tailbone (coccyx).

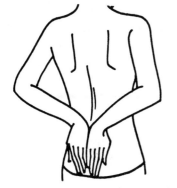

59

Positions for Treating Healee's Head

POSITION #1:

The heels of the hands are placed at the top of the forehead (hair-line) with the index fingers and thumbs abutted. Place the hands gently on the healee's face.

Remember to place a tissue over the eyes without covering the nose.

Specific imbalances being treated:*

Eye problems; sinus blockage;headache;migraines; stroke; allergies; upper respiratory congestion; hay fever; gum problems; toothache.

Glands: Pituitary (3rd Eye); Thalamus

POSITION #2:

Place the heels of the hands (at the wristline) on the crown of the head with the hands resting on the skull. The fingers extend towards the ears.

Specific imbalances being treated:

Mental organization and disorders; head injuries; stroke; stress; in coordination of left and right hemispheres of the brain; motor and thinking functions; headaches; migraines.

Glands: Pineal ; Hypothalamus

POSITION #3:

Fingertips are touching the lower edge of the skull (occipital bones) with the hands together on the back of the head.

Specific imbalances being treated:

Headaches; stroke; eye problems; nose bleeding (use ice pack); migraines; head injuries.

* "Specific Imbalances" are listed for purposes of education.

POSITION #4:

When treating while sitting at the head of the healee:

Place heels of hands slightly above the neckline, index fingers and thumbs together while hands rest on the upper chest region.

When treating while sitting on healee's right side:

LH: heel at throat with fingers pointed down on chest.
RH: fingertips at throat and heel of hand on chest.

Glands: Thyroid and parathyroids; Thymus

Specific imbalances being treated:

Energy stimulation; stress; immune; weight control; calcium absorption; Etheric heart: God-Self; nervousness; metabolism.

POSITION #1A:

Treat breast as needed.

Specific imbalances:

Cyst, tumors, lymphatic disorders, lactation disorders, pain during menstrual cycle, migraine head aches, ovarian or menstrual cycle imbalances.

*NOTE: Do not let hand contact the breast in treating women.

POSITION #1:

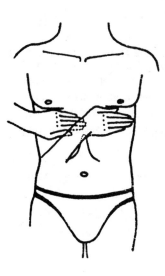

LH: placed under the breast line on the healee's right side.

RH: placed under the breast line on the healee's left side. Heel of hand touching the middle fingertip of LH.

Specific imbalances and areas being treated:

Right side: lower lungs; liver disorders: infections, blood sugar imbalances, blood disorders, digestion problems.

Left side: lower lungs; immune system: Spleen; gas release from heart region with heart trauma clients.

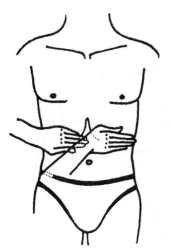

POSITION #2:

Move hands one hand-width down the body.

Specific imbalances and areas being treated:

Right side: vegetable protein digestion; gallbladder: gallstones; upper colon: colitis; constipation, mucus accumulation.

Left side: upper colon; stomach disorders, ulcers, spasms and digestive problems; pancreas: diabetes, blood sugar imbalances, hemophilia.

POSITION #3:

Again, move a hand-width down.

Specific imbalances being treated:

Right and left side: colon and upper small intestines; colitis, digestion, constipation, diverticulitis, stress (solar plexus) mucus accumulation, assimilation of nutrients from foods.

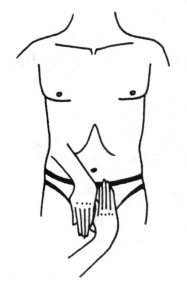

POSITION #4:

LH: fingers above pubic bone with hand medial to the hip bone.

RH: heel of the hand is above the pubic bone with hand medial to the hip bone.

Specific areas, organs, and imbalances being treated: lower small intestines and colon; bladder: infections, arthritis, cystitis; vagina and uterus: menstrual problems, infections; ovaries: cyst, menstrual cycle regulation dysfunctions, migraines; fallopian tubes. Remember that reproductive dysfunctions correlate with the Pituitary-Pineal and Adrenal glands.

*NOTE: Do not make contact with the reproductive areas. Allow your hands to be supported by your arms over and slightly away from, and not touching the reproductive areas of the healee's body.

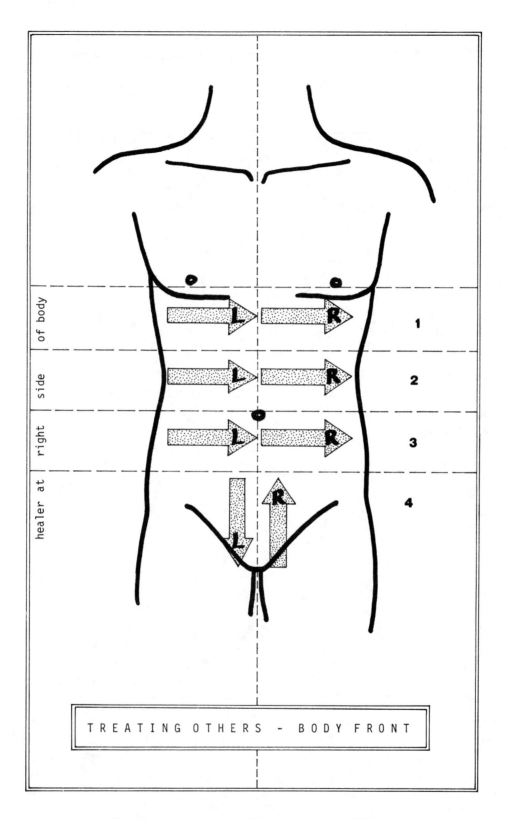

Treating Others - Arrow Diagram - Front of Body

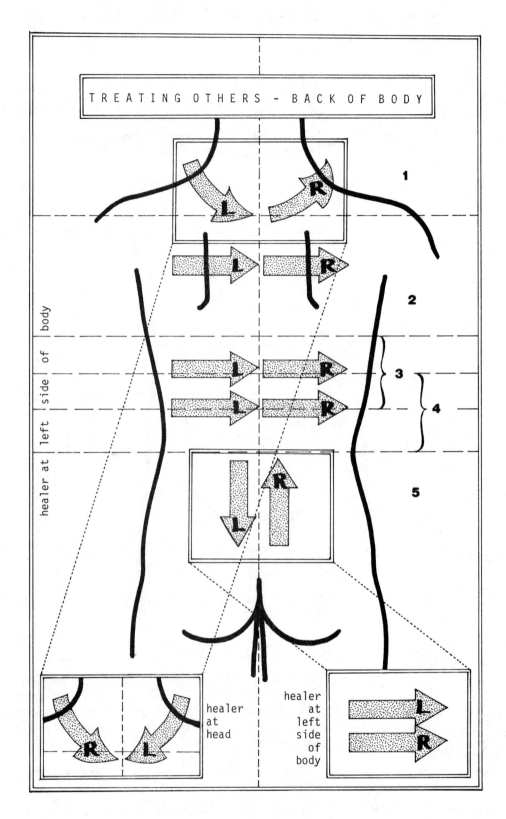

Treating Others - Back of Body

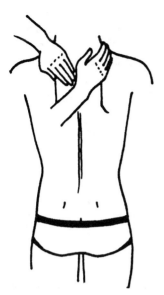

POSITION #1:

LH: the heel of the hand is on the upper part of the trapezius muscle and the middle fingertip is touching the side of the spine;

RH: the fingertips are on the shoulder muscle and the heel of the hand is touching the side of the spine.

Specific areas and imbalances being treated:

Tension; throat problems; spinal problems; headaches resulting from neck tension, ribhead dislocation in upper thorax misalignments.

POSITION #2:

LH: on the left shoulder blade.

RH: on the right shoulder blade.

Specific areas and imbalances being treated:

Nervousness; tension; back of lungs; spinal problems.

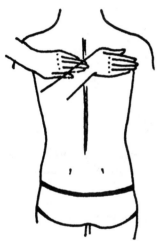

POSITION #3:

LH: over the left adrenal gland and the upper portion of that kidney.

RH: over the right adrenal gland and the upper portion of that kidney.

Specific imbalances being treated:

Diabetes; hypo- or hyperglycemia (blood sugar imbalances); stress; migraines; male or female reproductive problems; infections. Basically all body imbalances will require the need of additional treatment time on the adrenal glands. Treat Adrenal glands for, or to prevent, SHOCK.

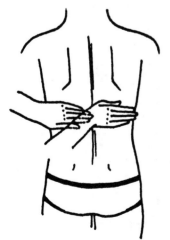

POSITION #4: hands are covering kidneys.

Specific imbalances being treated: kidney problems; arthritis; edema; high blood pressure; infections (to increase the filtering of toxins from the body by increasing kidney functions, also increase water consumption.)

POSITION #5:

LH: pointed down to tail bone;

RH: pointing up from tail bone.

Specific imbalances being treated: intestinal disorders; lumbar and sacral.

Special Positions for Specific Imbalances:

EARACHES: HEARING LOSSES: DEAFNESS (OTHERS):

Place the middle fingers gently in the ear opening. The middle finger will be bent to accomplish this. The index finger is placed on the head in front of the ear, while the ring and little fingers are placed behind the ear on the head.

Remember to treat under the jaw for earaches, as the auditory (eustachian) tubes may fill up with pus, fluid and mucus.

Treating Ears (Others):

Treating Eustachian Tubes (Others):

Treating Ears (Self):

Treating Eustachian Tubes (Self):

HIGH or LOW BLOOD PRESSURE, STROKES AND MIGRAINES:

Place one hand on the back of the head in the #3 Position, while the other hand rests <u>gently</u> on the side of the neck over the carotid artery. Treat until the energy flow stabilizes and then place hands in reversed positions.

SPECIAL NOTE: In cases of very high blood pressure (pressure above 180), I suggest that you begin treatment with the hand placed on the neck and then off the neck for 30 second intervals. Increase the time on the neck each time you place the hand on the neck during the treatment. The length of time for this treatment position is until the energy is balanced. This precaution will prevent a radical change in the blood pressure, which could cause faintness and nausea.

Treating Others (Rear View):   Treating Self (Side View): treat both sides

Treating Others (Side View):

SPECIAL POSITIONS FOR SPECIFIC IMBALANCES

IMMUNE SYSTEMS STIMULATION

TREATING OTHERS:

Place the LH on the thymus (at junction of the 3rd rib and the sternum you will find a small opening just below where the ribs attach to the breast bone.

Place the RH on the Spleen (#2 Position left-hand side of the body).

TREATING SELF

Place LH on Thymus

Place RH on Spleen

VARICOSE VEINS AND POOR CIRCULATION:

Your hands will be required to alternate to treat the left leg and then the right leg. Do not make contact with the clients reproductive organs.

Sitting on the right side of the patient, put your LH on the right side of his body in Position #4 and place your right hand so that it covers the groin. The hand should abut the line where the thigh and trunk are joined(the palm of the hand covers the inseam line, which places the palm over the femoral artery). Then place the RH on left side of body in Position #4, and the left hand on the left leg.

It is necessary for the healee to spread his or her legs to provide room to place your hand. Loose-fitting clothing or slacks are best. Treatment is for the length of time required to warm the healee's feet. Treat directly over the areas where varicose veins are ruptured, visible near the surface of the skin or painful.

Treating a Client: Treating Self:

CIRCULATION OF THE ARMS:

Place hands under the arm pits to increase the blood circulation to the arms.

Treating of lymphatic glands in this area is excellent for toxic build up and for cysts in the arm pit.

TREATING SELF:

Circulation

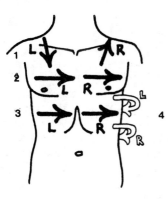

RESPIRATORY DYSFUNCTIONS:

Place the LH on right side as indicated by Arrows

Place the RH on the left side as indicated by Arrows

BACK OF LUNGS:

Place the LH on the left-hand side of the body and the RH on the right-hand side. Then, move down one hand-width each time to cover the lower portion of the lungs.

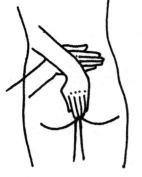

Treat also the sides of the lungs: it is easier to treat the left side of the person when he is face up and the right side when he is face down. This way you only have to reach across and place your hands side-by-side in the arm pit.

Remember to **never** place a patient with pneumonia face down. You will have to treat the back by reaching under and behind it. Incline the patient approximately 30 degrees up from the supine position.

PROSTATE (in men) and HEMORRHOIDS (men and women):

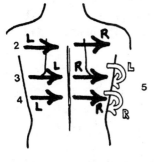

Place your LH over the centerline of the base of the spine (sacral bone) with the fingers pointed down and with the **tip of the middle finger** touching the anus opening outside through the clothing. The client should not wear panty hose, tight slacks or jeans.

The RH is placed across the lower back along the waistline underneath the left hand: A "T" formation.

TO REDUCE STRESS & INCREASE HEALEE'S ENERGY :

Place LH over the thyroid gland at the base of the throat.

Place the RH over the solar plexus (center of the body with hand above the navel upward to the diaphragm).

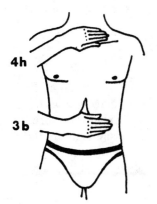

Positions 4H & 3B are excellent for Energy and Waking Up in the morning. The Reiki energy couples with the innate intelligence of the thyroid and adrenal glands, stimulating the necessary hormones to increase energy or to release stress and pain.

TO REDUCE STRESS & INCREASE YOUR ENERGY

Place LH over the thyroid gland at the base of the throat.

Place the RH over the solar plexus (midline of the body with hand above the navel upward to the diaphragm).

Positions 4H & 3B are excellent for Energy and Waking Up in the morning.

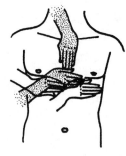

HEART PROBLEMS:

In all cases of heart imbalances, except heart attacks, you must first work in Position #1 to release the gas surrounding the heart. When the gas is released, then place both hands over the heart. (Shaded hand position.)

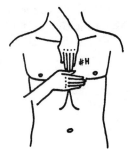

HEART ATTACKS:

Go directly to the heart. If the heart is not beating and if, and only if, you are trained in CPR you should attempt CPR. If breathing has ceased then begin resuscitation with one hand on the heart. Reiki has been known to revive the heart.

SPINAL PROBLEMS:

Scoliosis (any lateral curvature of the spine); arthritis; whiplash and related spinal injuries.

Place the LH on the shoulder in Position #1 on the left side of the spine.

Place the RH in the adjacent #1 Position.

Treat down the entire spinal column from Position #2 until reaching the #5 Position.

Spinal injuries will require lengthy sessions repeatedly.

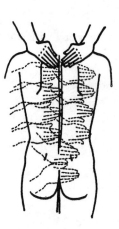

Spinal disorders have emotional and mental conflicts stored in the nerve and soft tissue surrounding the spine and adjacent muscles. The spinal technique SAT^{sm} is effective in clearing the stored trauma. Once the trauma is removed from the tissue memory the body will strengthen and the disorder will begin to heal. SAT^{sm} is an advanced 2nd and 3rd Degree technique developed by David Jarrell.

70

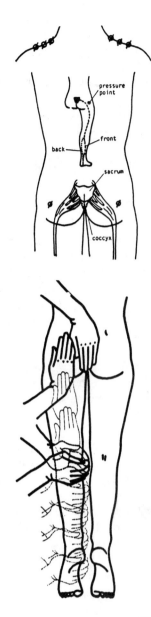

SCIATICA:

Neurological diagram of the sciatic nerve from the sacrum down the legs.

Note pressure points at shoulder: check these as indicators; also the pressure points in the dimple of the buttocks.

Sciatica is best treated in conjunction with Directional Non-Force chiropractic and **Spinal Attunement Technique**^{sm}, **Psycho-Therapeutic Reiki**^{sm}. First Degree is effect in pain control, but may not provide the emotional and structural alignment necessary for a complete healing. **SAT**^{sm} is co-taught by the author and Dr. Michael Weintraub.

A Spinal/Sacral balancing with a Cranial adjustment before receiving a First Degree Reiki treatment improves the healing of Sciatica.

SCIATICA TREATMENT:

Place the LH over the sacral bone with the fingers pointed down to the tip of the tail bone (coccyx).

With the RH, treat down the thigh (left and then the right), starting with the hand on the buttocks. When you reach the knee, bring the left hand down so you can sandwich the front and back of the lower leg (calf) and treat to the bottom of the foot.

FEMALE REPRODUCTIVE DISORDERS:

Place LH over the pubic/uterine area (Position #4). Place RH, without touching, between the legs with the palm of hand about an inch away from and in front of vaginal area. **The Client is to remain clothed during all Reiki treatments.**

Specific Imbalances: Yeast infections, herpes, vaginitis, cystitis, urinary tract disorders, menstrual complication and irregularities, ovulation disorders or bladder problems.

TREATING A CLIENT: TREATING SELF

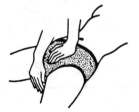

SINUS PRESSURE POINTS:

A. Place fingertips in notches on the upper orbital ridge of the eyebrow line; then,

B. Place index fingertips in center of lower orbital margin.

Reiki energy combined with gentle pressure helps to break up congestion in the sinuses

FIRST AID:

Always check for Breathing, Bleeding, and Shock. Never move or attempt to lift an injured person because of possible damage to the spinal column. Call for medical assistance immediately. Never leave an injured person once assistance is rendered, until relieved by qualified medical personnel.

LH: Place on injured area of the body.

RH: Placed on the adrenal glands (Position #3, hand centered across spine) to prevent shock. If victim is supine, then place hand on the solar plexus to relieve stress in the adrenals.

SANDWICHING AN INJURY:

Treating a wound, broken bone (through cast), muscle tissue, or burn.

Broken bones need to be aligned and set before healing directly over the break. You may treat around the area to control swelling, bleeding and pain. We do have reports where broken bones were treated with Reiki before being set with the bone aligning itself; however, the author does not have sufficient evidence of this always working so please follow the above instructions.

In treating burns it is best to keep the burn covered until your hands cease to send the Reiki energy, which will continue after the elimination of the persons pain.

TREATING THE FEET AND ANKLES

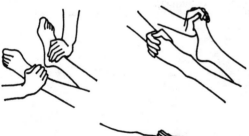

GROUNDING AFTER A HEALING:
Touch your fingertips together to break the magnetic charge between you and the healee. Wash your hands and arms in cool water after completing the healing to discharge any collected energy in your auric field.

SEQUENCE OF SELECTED POSITIONS IN A HEALING SESSION

POSITION #1 - HEAD

POSITION #1 - FRONT OF BODY

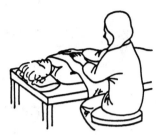

POSITION #1 - BACK

MAINTAINING AURIC FIELD CONTACT
Keep contact with healee when changing position

GROUP ATTUNEMENT AND HEALING

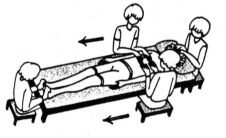

Left hand: Receives energy

Right hand: Gives energy

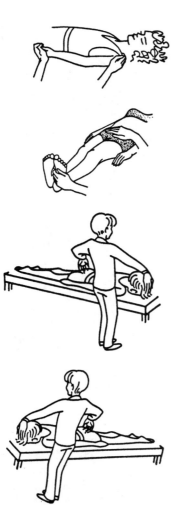

Specific conditions include: arthritis; broken bones; immune system: infections, cancer and AIDS. The Reiki energy will stimulate the bone marrow to produce white blood cells which then go to the spleen where a hormone from the thymus confers "immunologic competence" to the cell, now a "T" cell.

Broken leg, immune stimulation for all types of infections, arthritis of knee, hip and ankle.

LOWERING BODY ENERGY:

Reduces hypertension, excess energy, over expanded auric field and feelings of hyper-sensitivity.

RH: placed on Crown (fontanel).
LH: middle finger on coccyx

RAISING BODY ENERGY:

RH: Tip of middle finger touches the coccyx.

LH: Just off the head above the fontanel.

Specifics: Increases energy through spine housed within the CNS.

RELEASING SPINAL TENSION: Sequence of positions for releasing neuromuscular tension: process expands spinal disc spacing between the vertebrae for relaxation of spine.

Step #1: LH: Occiput (thumb and middle finger); RH: Coccyx (middle finger). Remain in this position until your pulse is synchronized between fingers of each hand.

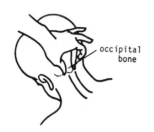

LH: Occiput position of spinal balancing diagram
from preceding page for the LH.

RELEASING SPINAL TENSION:

Step #2: Now, with your left hand at the neck and right hand on sacrum, move hands equally towards center of spine, one hand distance each move. Each move is completed when the pulse felt in your middle fingers is synchronized. It is the pulse of the dura membrane fluid.

Your hands never lose contact with the client's body during movement: "inch worm" your hands by pulling the heels to the fixed position of the middle finger, then sliding your fingers towards the center of the back while still touching the spine.

Now, if the spinal imbalance or pain is other than in the center of spine, you do the following: move the hand which is the farthest from the imbalance along the spine, one move at a time, allowing pulse synchronization, until the fingertips of your two hands are at equal distances from the point of imbalance; then, move both hands equal distance towards this point until the middle fingers are above and below the vertebra. It is not desired to have the tips of your middle fingers directly contacting the imbalanced vertebrae.

Concluding the Reiki treatment with the spinal technique is not only a means to reestablish neuro-muscular balance for proper distribution and transmission of physical energy, it adds the finishing touch to the Reiki treatment. Allow the client to remain on the healing table long enough to integrate the subtle healing energy into his or her physical body and conscious mind. Then help the client to roll on his or her side and assist them in sitting up. Please observe to what degree your client has established conscious contact with his or her body, since they may still need you physical assistance in standing up. Leaving your hand on the clients shoulder after helping them sit up, provides stability and grounding and a sense of security.

Be sure to make any notes in the clients files bases on your observations and registration of energy needs indicated by the amount of Reiki required to balance each part of the body. If the client volunteers comments about his or her experiences, visualizations and/or emotional awareness gained during the session, then record this information for future reference. Keeping thorough records help you to better assist the client in reaching his or her desired state of physical, emotional and mental wellness. It also establishes a professional relationship with your client and builds your data base of healing experiences.

INDEX

3rd chakra fear center, 33
3rd eye, 24, 25, 60

A

A pregnant woman will need, 46
A protective technique, 42
Acid, 25, 51
Acid metabolism, 51
Acute, 46, 47
Adrenal, 25, 26, 34, 69
Adrenal glands, 42, 62, 65, 72
Adrenals, 24, 34
AIDS, 74
Alcoholism, 35
Alkaline, 25
Alkaline metabolism, 51
Allergen, 48
Allergies, 60
Allergy, 48
Anger, 16, 17, 33, 36, 39
Anterior Lobe Pituitary, 26
Anus, 69
Arms, 72
Arthritis, 62, 66, 70, 74
Arthritis of knee
  hip and ankle, 74
Ascended Masters, 18, 22
Aspirant, 25
Assimilation of nutrients, 62
Atlas, 30
Attuned to the healee's pain, 41
Aura, 17, 31, 40
Auras instantly express, 44
Auric field, 13, 72, 73, 74
Awareness, 14, 15, 16, 17, 19, 20, 21, 25, 26, 31, 35, 39, 45, 47, 75

B

Baths for Detoxification and Pain, 48
Black candle, 44
Bladder problems, 71
Bleeding, 12, 72
Blood, 48, 50, 51
Blood disorders, 61
BLOOD PRESSURE, 67
Blood sugar imbalances, 62, 65
Blue, 12, 24
Brain, 17, 25, 32, 33, 34

Breast, 56
Broken bone, 72, 74
Burns, 72

C

Calcium, 34, 48, 51
Calcium absorption, 61
Calcium stones, 51
Cancer, 48, 74
Cayenne Pepper, 48
Chakra, 13, 26, 27, 28, 34, 36, 40, 44
Chakra balance, 39
Chakra bodies, 28
Christ, 13, 14, 16, 25, 46
Christ Conscious, 35
Christ Conscious Center, 25
Christ consciousness, 26, 31, 49
Christ Presence, 44
Chronic, 46
Circulation, 34
CIRCULATION OF THE ARMS, 68
Clairaudience, 25
Clairvoyance, 25
Clear Crystal, 24
Clitoris, 28
Clothing, 43
Coccyx, 24, 26, 28, 30, 59, 74
Colon, 48, 50, 51
Comfrey, 51
Comfrey-Fenugreek, 48
Comfrey-Pepsin, 48
Conditional love, 31
Conscious awareness, 42
Consciousness, 9, 13, 14, 15, 16, 17, 18, 19, 20, 25, 26, 28, 31, 33, 34, 35, 41
Constipation, 62
Cosmic fire, 24, 25, 26, 28
Co-creative, 14, 26, 35
Co-creative God consciousness, 25
Co-creative God-Presence, 41
CPR, 70
Cranial adjustment, 71
Creative distributor, 24
Creative Intellect, 26, 33
Creative mind, 26, 33
Crown chakra, 19, 21, 24, 25, 41, 74
Cumberland Institute for Wellness Education^{sm}, 20
Cyst, 61, 68
Cystitis, 62, 71
C/P Point, 28

D

Darkness cannot overshadow Light, 42
DEAFNESS, 66
Detoxify, 47
Diabetes, 62, 65
Digestion problems, 61
Directional Non-Force chiropractic, 71
Distribution of light, 28
Diverticulitis, 62
Divine Self, 41
Dr. Usui, 10, 11, 12, 13, 14, 19
Dura membrane fluid, 75

E

EARACHES, 66
Edema, 66
Eighth Chakra, 41
Emerald, 24
Emerald Ray, 9
Epson salts, 48
Etheric body, 25, 38
Etheric heart, 24, 61
Eustachian Tubes, 66
Expansion of consciousness, 21
Eye problems, 60

F

Fallopian tubes, 62
Fasting - Preparation, 50
Fear center, 41, 42
Feelings (energy) affect us on subjective levels, 42
FEMALE REPRODUCTIVE DISORDERS, 71
Femoral artery, 68
Fenugreek, 51
FIRST AID, 72
Flushing the Stones, 52
Fontanel, 74
Free will, 14, 32, 33

G

Gallbladder: gallstones, 62
Gallstones, 50, 51
God is in the heart, 36
God's Laws, 49
God-consciousness, 26
God-Self, 31, 36, 37, 61
Golden-White, 24
Grace, 32, 46
Green, 51
Green stringies., 51

GROUP ATTUNEMENT, 73
Guilt
  self-imposed or accepted, 38
Gum problems, 60

H

Hand Pressure, 45
Hay fever, 60
Headache, 60
Headaches resulting from neck tension, 65
Healing consciousness, 45
Healing state of mind, 43
HEARING LOSSES, 66
Heart, 9, 13, 14, 17, 19, 20, 21, 24, 25, 26, 31, 32, 34, 35, 36, 38, 39, 41, 44, 49
Heart attacks, 70
Heart chakra, 20, 27
HEART PROBLEMS, 70
Hemophilia, 62
Hemorrhoids, 69
Herpes, 71
High blood pressure, 66
Higher consciousness, 25
Higher self, 9, 23, 26, 33
His Divine Plan of Happiness
  Joy and Love, 41
His Perfect Image, 49
Holy Breath, 14, 41
How Often To Fast, 52
Hygiene, 43
Hypertension, 74
Hypoglycemia, 52
Hypothalamus, 26, 60

I

Imaging, 9
Imbalanced chakra, 38
Immune system, 25, 61, 74
IMMUNE SYSTEMS STIMULATION, 67
Inability to attain orgasm, 39
Incarnation, 32
INCREASE YOUR ENERGY, 70
Infections, 48, 65, 74
Initiations, 18, 19, 20, 21
Innate intelligence, 69
Insulin balance, 52
Intestinal disorders, 66
Intestines, 47, 48, 50, 51
Invite the Christ Presence into the Healing, 44
Invocation of Healing:, 44
I-Ego-ism, 15

K

Karma, 13, 15, 19
Kidney problems, 66
Kundalini, 26, 28, 34

L

Lactation disorders, 61
Left hemisphere, 25
Life Force, 16, 25, 26, 31, 39
Liver, 25, 26, 47, 50, 51
Liver disorders: infections
  blood sugar imbalance, 61
Living God consciousness, 40
Living-to-die consciousness, 36
Living-to-heal consciousness, 36
Low density lipid proteins, 35
Lower back problems, 46
LOWERING BODY ENERGY, 74
Lumbar, 66
Lungs, 47, 48, 61, 69
Lymph glands, 50, 51
Lymphatic disorders, 61
Lymphatic glands, 68
Lymphatic system, 47

M

Magnesium, 44
Massage Therapist, 20
Master's Candidate, 20
Meditation, 35
Melatonin, 35
Menstrual complication, 61, 71
Mental body, 19, 26, 34
Mental organization, 60
Metabolism, 61
Migraines, 39, 60, 61, 62, 65, 67
Mind, 9, 12, 14, 18, 19, 25, 32, 34
Mirrored responses, 49
Mother-Father God, 44
Mucous, 48, 50, 51
Mucus-forming foods, 50
Muscle pain, 48
Music, 43

N

Nervousness, 61, 65
Neurotransmitters, 33
Nose bleeding, 60
Nutritional deficiencies, 49

O

Occiput, 30, 53, 74, 75
Orange, 24
Ovarian or menstrual cycle imbalances, 61, 71
Ovaries, 24, 26, 39
Ovaries: cyst
  menstrual cycle regulation dysfunct, 62

P

Pancreas, 26, 62
Parathyroids, 24, 25, 26, 34, 61
Penis, 28
Pepsin, 51
Pineal gland, 19, 24, 25, 26, 28, 34, 35, 60, 62
Pink, 17, 24, 43
Pituitary, 19, 24, 25, 34, 60, 62
Pituitary imbalance, 39
Pneumonia, 69
POLARITY POSITIONS, 74, 75
POOR CIRCULATION, 68
Posterior Lobe Pituitary, 26
Prayer, 9, 44
Professional Practitioners Certification, 20
Professional relationship, 75
Proper energy shield, 42
Proper frequency of bowel movements, 50
Prostate, 26, 39, 69
PSEB[sm], 22
Psycho-physical, 25, 26, 33, 36, 42, 47, 48
Psycho-Therapeutic Reiki[sm] Healing, 19, 71
Purple, 24, 44
Pyramids of Light Inc., 22

R

RAISING BODY ENERGY, 74
Records, 75
Red, 24
REDUCE STRESS, 70
Reiki Plus   Institute's Professional Practitioners, 20
Reiki Plus   Mastership, 20
Reiki Plus   Practitioner, 41
Reiki Ray, 9, 10, 11, 19
Reiki slaw, 50, 51
RELEASING SPINAL TENSION, 74, 75
Reproductive, 24, 34
Reproductive problems, 65
RESPIRATORY DYSFUNCTIONS, 69
Ribhead dislocation, 65
Right hemisphere, 25
Root chakra, 21, 24, 26, 28
Rose red, 24
R.P.I, 20

S

Sacred self, 28
Sacrum, 24, 26, 30,66, 71, 75
Salt-soda bath, 48
SAT^{sm}, 70
SCIATICA, 71
Second chakra, 45
Second Degree of the **Reiki Plus** system, 19
Seventh chakra, 19
Sexual center, 26
SHOCK, 65, 72
Sinus, 60
SINUS PRESSURE POINTS, 72
Sixth chakra, 19, 39
Sixth etheric body, 41
Skin, 47
Spleen, 24, 25, 26, 61, 74
Solar plexus, 24, 26, 42, 69, 70, 72
Soul consciousness, 34
Soul's journey, 32, 40
Spinal Attunement Technique^{sm}, 71
Spinal disc spacing, 74
Spinal problems, 65
Spine, 9, 26, 28, 69, 70, 72, 74, 75
Spiritual consciousness, 40
Spiritual illumination, 32
Spiritual Sight, 25
Starting up the Motor, 47
Stomach disorders, 62
Stress, 62
Stroke, 60, 67
Subtle body, 34
Sub-Acute, 46
Swollen tissue, 48

T

Testes, 24, 26
Thalamus, 60
The Fasting Foods, 50
The Fasting Steps, 51
The Healer's attunement, 44
The treatment, 44
THE TWENTY-ONE DAY HEALING CYCLE, 21
Think the color pink, 45
Third chakra, 34
Third degree burns, 45
Third Degree Practitioner, 20
Thought-forms, 34, 36, 37, 40, 47, 48, 49
Throat chakra, 19, 24, 25, 33, 34, 36, 38, 39
Throat problems, 65
Thymus, 24, 25, 26, 28, 34, 35, 61, 74
Thyroid, 19, 24, 25, 26, 34, 61, 69, 70
Tissue memory, 70

Toothache, 60
Touching: A professional attitude, 45
Toxic thoughts of guilt and fear, 49
Toxicity - Purification Process, 47
Toxin removal, 47
Toxins, 47, 66
Treating an open infection, 43
Trials of Fire, 25
Tumors, 61

U

Ulcers, 62
Unconditional love, 9, 13, 18, 24, 38, 40
Undeveloped consciousness, 24
Universal laws, 9
Unresolved stress, 46
Unwellness is unbalanced energy, 46
Upper colon: colitis; constipation mucus accumula, 62
Urinary tract disorders, 71
Uterine, 71

V

Vagina and uterus: menstrual problems infections, 62
Vaginitis, 71
VARICOSE VEINS, 68
Vertebrae, 30, 34, 74, 75
Violation of the law, 22
Vital heart, 24

W

Water, 50, 51
Weight control, 61
When you finish the fast, 51
White blood cells, 74
White candle, 44
White cocoon, 42
White Light, 12, 25, 35, 42

Y

Yang, 25, 37
Yeast infections, 71
Yellow, 24
Yin, 25, 37

"Flame of God's Light.", 44
"immunologic competence", 74
"Let go and Let God.", 46
"Original Sin.", 49
"T" cell, 74

RPI Crossover Policy

Welcome All Students of Reiki.
We invite you to Audit Reiki Plus® First and Second Degree Classes

Let us remember what the Zen Monk said to Dr. Usui..." All are welcomed who wish to learn.
Please come and study with us and fulfill your destiny."

<u>AUDIT</u>:   If you are already a student of the Usui System of Reiki Natural Healing, you are welcomed to *Audit* a **Reiki Plus®** First or Second Degree Class. **You must have been initiated** by a Teacher of Reiki to the Degree Level you wish to Audit. Certification of Training, showing date and Teacher is required as proof of Initiation to level you are requesting to audit. Otherwise, Tuition will be **$200.00** (early Registration - $175.00) for First Degree and $500.00 (early Registration $450.00) for Second Degree **Reiki Plus.** Books cost $15.00 for First Degree and $33.00 for Second Degree.

<u>PRICE: (For Audit only)</u>

Reiki Plus Second Degree $250.00: the Reiki Student learns the unique technique to heal the Causal Factor, we call it **Psycho-Therapeutic Reiki**sm Healing, and gains a working knowledge of the Etheric and Chakra Bodies affected by the imbalances of the of the individual's mind, body and emotions.

A student Auditing either class will receive credit hours in the Institute if and when they become enrolled in the Institute as a student of either of the 3 Certification Programs. Please see the **Reiki Plus Institute's** Catalogue. They will of course be awarded, a Certificate of completion , for any course taken in the Institute.

We invite you and/or your community of Reiki students to investigate and explore the **Reiki Plus Institute's** program. We look forward to providing you and your friends the professional education necessary to become a Professional Practitioner of Natural Healing using functional energy. Let us remember that our spiritual union and bonding exists through our ties with the teachings of Reiki, already they unite us on the energy planes of healing.

PLEASE PRINT OR TYPE IN BLACK INK. THANK YOU

Name_____ phone (_____) _____

Address_____State_____ Zip _____

Please : I am A Reiki I [ ] Reiki II [ ], Trained by Reiki Master_____,

I WOULD LIKE TO ORDER:

1. Catalogue(s) _____at $3.00 each;   (Make checks payable to **Pyramids of Light Inc.**)

2. Teachers and Centers can order Books in Quantity : Please Call or write for discount.

<u>CHECK   THE APPROPRIATE BOXES BELOW</u>

5. **I am a Networker and** would like to sponsor a Reiki Plus Class. Please send me information about how I can become a Sponsor. (Sponsors can earn their education in exchange for the work required as a Sponsor.) _____

6. I am interested in becoming a student of **Reiki Plus** and have not taken Reiki Training. Please have a Teacher of the Institute contact me   [   ] or I would like to know how I can Sponsor a RPI Teacher in my area [   ].

7. **I am a Reiki Teacher** interested in becoming trained in **Reiki Plus** [   ], to become a Certified Teacher of **Reiki Plus** [   ]

Reiki Plus Institute & Reiki Plus Publications
Rt. 3 Box 313, Celina, TN. 38551, Ph/fax (615) 243-3712

Classes Developed and Taught by David G. Jarrell

Reiki Plus ® First Degree   Credit Hours   20
Prerequisites: Desire to be responsible for oneself and accepting of God's unconditional love.
This seminar is designed to teach techniques to use with the self and with clients to promote healing, relaxation and the reduction of stress.   This class is highly experiential   to provide hands on contact for you to truly know what Reiki energy feels like. Students give and receive a group treatment. Spontaneous healings are common.

Learn how to: Activate, direct and apply Reiki healing to self and others; Apply hand positions for giving a total body Reiki treatment; Appreciate the human energy system with its natural restorative and balancing mechanisms; Understand how Reiki is an independent healing system, as well as an adjunct to all healing processes; Identify hand positions to be used with selected pathology problems; Understand that Reiki is a self growth tool facilitating personal wellness of mind, body & emotions; Receive the Four Initiations for Attunement to the First Degree level of Reiki Energy.

Reiki Plus® Second Degree   Credit Hours   15
         Receive the attunement to the Second Degree Level of Reiki Energy. Learn how Second Degree is combined with mystical teachings. Activate, direct and apply Second Degree energy to self, fellow students and to clients. Learn several Distant Healing techniques and experience a heightened intuitive sensitivity developed by Distant Healing. Learn the Affirmation Technique to relieve stress and support desired changes in the life of your client.

Advanced _Reiki Plus_®   Second Degree   Credit Hours   15

Prerequisites: Second Degree student receive at least **1 Psycho- Therapeutic Reiki**^{sm} Treatment..
 Identify psycho-physical, emotional and mental disorders with which Second Degree is an appropriate holistic intervention. Learn how to identify which **Psycho-Therapeutic Reiki**^{sm}Technique will best assist the client to   create a receptive conscious mind in order to   accept God's Forgiveness and healing Light. Learn the three **Psycho-Therapeutic Reiki**^{sm} Techniques to remove stored trauma and dis-ease from the chakras and the physical body.
Practicum: Receive and Perform a minimum of 3 healings of **Psycho-Therapeutic Reiki**^{sm} to receive Certificate of completion.

Esoteric Psychology (f/k/a APHA I)   Available **only by Home Study Tape**.   Credit Hours   20
         The student will learn   procedures to assess the client for obtaining the thesis of the client's psycho-physical challenge. Techniques to develop insight to <u>see</u> the subtle implications presented by the client's words describing the conditions (symptoms). The proper listening to the client's <u>words</u> and description of conditions will provide delineation and synthesis.   The reward of this technique is learning how to redirect the psycho-physical towards wellness and the ability to cope without debilitating stress. **A prerequisite for all advance courses in the RPI.**

Esoteric Anatomy (f/k/a APHA 2   Available **only by Home Study Tapes**   Credit Hours   20
         This second class takes **Esoteric Psychology** to an applied approach, teaching the Healing Arts Practitioner the fundamental tools of Esoteric Anatomy and Psychology.   The technique is for integrating subjective symptoms through intuitive observation by the Practitioner. The student learns a comprehensive knowledge of the chakra bodies (etheric bodies) and their neurological connection to the glands and organs. **A prerequisite for all advance courses in the RPI.**

Advanced Psycho-Therapeutic^{sm} Reiki (f/k/a APHA 3) on Home Study Tapes   Credit Hours   25
 Student must have completed a minimum of 15 **Psycho-Therapeutic Reiki**^{sm} sessions. The student will understand kundalini, be able to interpret imbalanced energy distribution. and recognize dysfunctional color when present in an organ or part of the anatomy. The student becomes proficient in the **Creative Distributor Technique^{sm}** for releasing psycho-physical, emotional and mental trauma.

Applied Psychology of Healing Anatomy   Prerequisites: **APHA 3** Credit Hours   25
The student will learn to further his technique of interpreting how the psycho-physical, psycho-emotional and psycho-mental speak through the anatomy. **The Intuitive Therapeutic Approach**^{sm}, **TITA**^{sm} Technique, develops the Practitioners knowledge of color and chakra function to facilitate a release of the trauma retained in the tissue. The student will gain an understanding and learn guidance from color, which allows the   psycho-emotional memory to reveal the 3 levels of stored trauma of a stress pattern, emotional or mental dysfunction, addiction or disease.

SAT^{sm} Prerequisites: Second Degree, Esoteric Psychology and Anatomy & PSEB^{sm}   Credit Hours 25
         The **Spinal Attunement Technique^{sm}** is the method of non-manipulative alignment of the sacral-spinal-occiput components of the skeletal system by advanced **Psycho-Therapeutic Reiki**^{sm} energy work. If the psycho-physical, psycho-emotional and psycho-mental trauma is released from the spinal complex, the body and spine will heal. The student will learn how to clear the psycho-physical of the emotional and mental stress of a traumatic memory.

A

*PSEB*sm I (*Physio-Spiritual Etheric Body*sm healing)   Credit Hours   20

This etheric body healing technique unites the *physical and etheric bodies* to allow spiritual harmony to flow through them from God. Harmony must exist in this domain to establish and maintain wellness. The student learns: the basic concepts of Psycho-anatomy linking the biomagnetic functions of the soma; to develop intuition and sensitivity to feel the bio-electrical currents and the polarity of the eight major body vortexes; to distinguish and align the imbalanced electrical currents within the biomagnetic field; learn an effective and safe technique to work in the biomagnetic fields; and to align and stimulate the biomagnetic energy flow to the soma from the chakras, the subtle bodies, thus, creating a healing environment for the physical body.

Intuitive Evaluation of Client Consciousness (see page C)   (Available on Home Study Tapes) Credit Hours   20

Individual's confront the challenges of everyday life from the level of maturity and insight they have acquired. How an individual confronts a life challenge equates the level of trauma stored in the unconscious mind and tissue of the body. The individual's response or reaction is a result of genetics, parental and social conditioning and expectations. When an individual has gained an understanding of the "why now" syndrome, he can assess his psycho-emotional and psycho-mental response or reaction. Clarity requires understanding of the reasons the personality chose the challenges for his Ego's growth towards Soul Consciousness.

Healing takes place through forgiveness, surrender and faith that the Ego is learning to be a better Christ conscious person. This personality is seeking greater recognition of life's reason. This is so because the person has chosen to change his personality by learning the refined insight from his lessons. We have determined there to be Ten Levels of Consciousness that the personality must traverse to prepare itself for this task. This class provides the student the training to assess the client's level of consciousness.

Astro-Physiology and Psychology I (see page C)   (Available by Home Study Tapes)   Credit Hours   50

The student is first given an Astrological foundation from the spiritual and Transpersonal perspective. Then has incorporated Astro-physiological and psychological interpretation of the chakra/etheric body anatomy and the potential manifestations chosen to challenge the ego's union with soul consciousness. Learn spinal analysis, recognition of physical and psychological disorders and how to help your client with his or her challenges. Course also covers delineation of Natal Aspects, Transit, Progressions, and Cycles from the Spiritual and Personality structure of the ego. Booklet of study material is provided with this course to aid your study of the charts interpreted in the course. David has over 22 years professional experience as an Astrologer giving Astro-Spiritual Profiles for clients around the world.

Reiki Plus® Third Degree Practitioner   Credit Hours   30

David G. Jarrell is the only **Reiki Master** who Initiates qualified students to this level of *Reiki Plus*. Third Degree increases the depth, intensity and effectiveness of the Practitioner's healing work. The life transformations can take up to 1 year to integrate as the cyclical changes are more rapid and have the potential to awaken your awareness of lifes multiple dimensions co existing simultaneously.

Reiki Master Training

A. To begin training for **Reiki Master** to Teach *Reiki Plus* First and Second Degree the student must be invited by David G. Jarrell. Then the student must complete the **Advance *Reiki Plus*® Practitioner's** Program, be an Ordained Minister of Healing in the Pyramids of Light Church and complete the Reiki Master's Candidate training and obligations of contract.

B. To be initiated to **Reiki Master to teach traditional Reiki** First and Second Degree, the student must show professional ability and aptitude in teaching, as well as a proficiency in his or her personal Reiki practice. The **standard requirements of Takata and my Teacher, Virginia Samdahl, is to have treated at least 100 different clients with different disorders**. Initiation to **Reiki Master** is earned after successful completion of training and payment of tuition.

•   If a candidate has parallel professional training, Degrees and experience, requirements will be waived on an individual basis.

C. **Reiki Master Crossover Training.** An existing **Reiki Master** who has been trained in the pure lineage of the Usui System of Natural Healing and is interested in cross training to become a **Reiki Master certified and licensed to teach *Reiki Plus* First and Second Degree** is invited to communicate directly with David G. Jarrell. Please write to the Institute.

Reiki Plus® Institute, Rt. 3 Box 313, Celina, TN 38551 Ph/Fax (615) 243-3712

Reiki Plus® *Institute*
Seminars for Professional Training on Audio Cassette
All Tapes from actual classes taught by David G. Jarrell

1.   **Esoteric Psychology** (f/k/a APHA 121)   **$125.00 - 20 Credit Hours.**   **6 - 90" Tapes**
Esoteric Psychology, the visible and invisible aspects of the Practitioner and Client precounseling interview; the healer-Healee relationship; and, how to custom design your Practitioner's Interview Form. A 12 page Booklet is included for following the Course Lecture Material

2.   **Esoteric Anatomy** (f/k/a APHA 122)   **$125.00 - 20 Credit Hours.**   **6 - 90" Tapes**
Esoteric Anatomy - understanding how the Personality vs. the Spiritual consciousness must be approached to properly interpret a client's process of challenge. A 17 page Booklet is included for following the Course Lecture Material.

3.   **Advanced Psycho-Therapeutic Reiki** (f/k/a APHA 223): **$205.00 - 20 Credit Hours. 6 - 90" Tapes**
Learn the advance *Creative Distribution Technique* developed from David Jarrell's extensive healing work with the *Psycho-Therapeutic Reiki*sm Technique. You will learn the sacrum's involvement in the distribution of light
for a healthy body-mind-emotions balance. This training will provide you an understanding to work with deeper rooted imbalances and disorders, while learning an entirely new way of mapping the imbalanced energy in the clients' body.

4.   **Astro-Physiology and Anatomy 581**   **$300.00 - 50 Credit Hours.**   **21 - 90" Tapes**
    Available in individual Segments 1, 2, & 3: -7 tapes each set for $125.00
The student is first given an Astrological foundation from the spiritual and Transpersonal perspective. Then has incorporated Astrophysiological and psychological interpretation of the chakra/etheric body anatomy and the potential manifestations chosen to challenge the ego's union with soul consciousness. Learn spinal analysis, recognition of physical and psychological disorders and how to help your client with his or her challenges. Course also covers delineation of Natal Aspects, Transit, Progressions, and Cycles from the Spiritual and Personality structure of the ego. Booklet of study material is provided with this course to aid your study of the charts interpreted in the course. David has over 23 years professional experience as an Astrologer giving Astro-Spiritual Profiles for clients around the world.

5.   **IECC 163** (Master's of the Ten Rays in your Aura):   **$125.00 - 20 Credit Hours**   **6 - 90" Tapes**
Inner Evaluation of Client Consciousness and the evolution of the Soul's journey to infuse with Spiritual Christ Consciousness. A powerful class containing essential material for spiritual healing. Learn what the colors surrounding your clients and friends really means. Know what Ray they are evolving through and when they will finish the journey.

6.   **Transmutation Meditation Tape $10.00.**
7.   **Fairy Tale Regression (**side A) From Reiki I Class and an **Invocation of the Masters** (side B) **Tape $10.00.**

8.   *PSEB*sm *111 - New Study Tapes in the 1993 Class Format.* $75.00   **6 - 90" Tapes**
Must be Certified in PSEB   **to purchase these tapes.**

Students who purchase Seminars by Tape for Credit Hours may attend the Seminar for 2/3 rd's of the Seminar's Tuition.

To Place your order simply send money order payable to:
Reiki Plus Publications,
Rt 3 Box 313, Celina, TN 38551,

All Orders over $100.00 shipped Free.
Single Tapes shipped 4th Class Mail,; $2.00 first tape, 50¢ each additional Tape. **NO UPS t o PO Box's**
MC/Visa, add 5% Service Charge to your order .   Card orders may be placed by phone 615/243-3712.

Print:
Name _____Phone #_____

Address _____
City_____State _____Zip _____

VISA/MC #_____ Expiration date_____

Name on Card_____Signature_____

Tape Set(s)by # :_____Cost of Sets $ _____Shipping $_____ Amount enclosed$_____

C

Reiki Plus® Publications

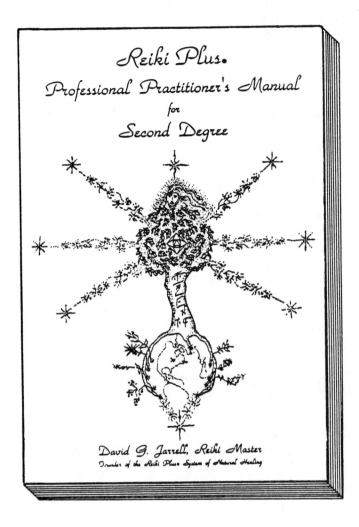

Reiki Plus® Professional Practitioner's Manual for Second Degree 1st Edition, by David G. Jarrell

Sub Titled **"What to do now, that I'm Reiki Two".**

The book Reiki Students around the world have been waiting to read. The Professional reference material necessary to guide all students of Reiki and other modalities of healing in their private healing practice.

Teaches guidelines to manage a professional practice, to use the energy of Reiki Second Degree to its potential, to send Distant Healing, plus other mystical techniques...it unveils the mysteries of Reiki Second Degree.

Chapter 6. covers Metabolic Nutrition by Dr. Richard Brodie, Ph.D., Psychologist and Nutritionist.

Chapter 7. is 43 pages, Listing over 80 Diseases or Disorders. Includes detailed information for Reiki Treatments, Nutrition, Herbs, Cell Salts, the "Probable Esoteric Psychological Cause" and the Chakras.

101 Pages   Acrylic coated Soft Cover, Perfect Bound

8½ X 11" Format for easy Reading and Reference.
Retails for : $22.00 ISBN 0-9634690-1-0

Reiki Plus® Professional Practitioner's Manual for Second Degree.

This book has evolved from the 12 years of teaching and private practice of David Jarrell.

Postage FREE via book mail.

Available at discount in quantity to Reiki Masters and Schools for Resale.

Send your check or Money Order payable to
Reiki Plus Publications, Rt 3 Box 313, Celina, TN 38551

Name_____phone (_____) _____

Address_____St_____ Zip_____

Number of Copies_____@ $22.00 *Reiki Plus Professional Practitioners Manual for Second Degree* $_____

Number of Copies_____@ $15.00 *Reiki Plus Natural Healing,* 4th Edition (1991) $_____

If you desire First Class shipping please add $2.00 per book. For Priority 2nd Day Mail add $3.00 per book.
Both may be ordered at a Savings of $2.00 when ordered together, Special price $35.00